Layouts to inspire

Compiled by Mike Marritt

Design and typesetting by Artytype

ISBN 978-0-9503217-8-3

Contents

Introduction

'**I**NSPIRE**'** – my copy of *The Concise Oxford Thesaurus* lists 'stimulate', 'motivate', 'encourage', 'influence', and 'fire the imagination' as alternative words that could be used instead.

I think that most, if not all of those words apply to the layouts featured in this book, and hope that readers will indeed be inspired to build a model railway of their own if they have not already done so.

This book is intended as a sequel to the *Small Layouts Volumes 1 and 2* previously published by the Gauge O Guild. This time the remit was to include layouts of all shapes and sizes, not just those modest in area, and I have been able to achieve that. The content has been selected or recommended solely by Guild members on the basis that they proved inspirational to their own efforts in the hobby.

What has become clear to me is that it is not necessarily a top quality layout that proves to be the most inspirational, although there are several in that category included herein. The layouts in this book include one built by a member with very limited eyesight, another by a modeller suffering from Parkinson's Disease, and a third built by a modeller who normally builds in 2mm scale but who built his first working 7mm model in just two months, with most of the layout scratch-built. All of these layouts have provided motivation to, and plaudits from, their modelling colleagues.

Sixty years ago a number of modellers gathered together to form the Gauge O Guild, at a time when the scale of 7mm to the foot was a scale used only by a very small number of aficionados. The ready to run models available were few and far between. A few devotees built their own stock from a very limited range of parts. Scenic layouts were very crude or non-existent.

Now that the Guild is entering it's seventh decade, I hope this book will show how much things have changed, and how successful the intervening years have been in improving railway modelling in 7mm. DCC is taking over from DC as the favoured power source. Many modellers now concentrate on building and operating layouts, and upgrading the commercial items now available. I believe that this success is due in no small measure to the existence and influence of the Gauge O Guild.

One final thought. Modellers must aim to continue improving their standards, in particular by using the most modern technology available. Each and every one of us should try to make the next big birthday of the Guild one where we can say that the quality of our models has improved to the extent that 2016 was merely a stop along the way to our personal idea of fulfilment.

Mike Marritt

I would like to thank Ade Haines and Artytype for their help,
advice and co-operation in the preparation of this book.
MM.

The Paddington Line *by Tony Crouch*

Photographs by Steve Flint courtesy of Railway Modeller

The Great Western Railway mainline in its heyday

The Paddington Line is a GWR (c1936) model railway that runs both indoors and outdoors. Construction began in 1990 with a design for the indoor section of the railway to fit the upper floor level of the double garage. The indoor section represents Paddington as well as a typical GW loco depot with some storage sidings for rolling stock. The railway accesses the outdoor section through an end wall and takes a 9ft radius curve, rising on a gradient of 1 in 70 due to the sloping terrain of the garden. The lines from the indoor section join a double track running circle on the level that includes a representation of Reading station and a junction for a single line branch. A single track reversing loop from the down main line enables return running into Paddington on the up main line.

The original electrics were designed for 12V DC with six Gaugemaster controls and many line sections controlled by six switchboards. During 2005 the whole system was converted to DCC using a Digitrax Super Chief system, which is divided, into four power districts. The reversing loop is supplied through a reversing unit.

DCC Systems

The master unit (DCS 100) is located within the indoor Paddington area, with the main track supply going out to a four district power management unit (PM42) located at St Margaret's Junction. This supplies the four power districts as follows:

1. Paddington area and the lines to St Margaret's Junction
2. Complete circuit from Old Oak Bridge to Reading East Junction
3. The Branch Line
4. Reading Station area

The reversing loop is supplied from power district number 2.

Track

Track, turnouts and crossings are entirely Peco. The point control system is entirely manual with levers activating microswitches to change frog polarity.

Indoors

The baseboard, at a height of 30in, is 28ft long and a 9ft wide, with operating spaces of 30in and 23in on either side.

Paddington Station

The platforms are constructed of ply and measure as follows:-

Platform	Length (ft)	Scale length (ft)	Real Paddington length (ft)
No 1	20	871	1150
No 2	19.5	849	1125
No 3	17.5	762	1125
No 4	17	740	1050
No 5	17	740	1050

There is a further platform No 6 for goods and parcels, adjacent to platform No 5 outside of the main roof structure, and also a platform No 1A, which is the equivalent of the parcels office at Paddington.

The station roof is constructed to Brunel's design. Each of the main sections measures 45in (scale 163ft) in length and 35in (scale 127ft) in width. The two transepts are also constructed to Brunel's design. The lawn area and roof have been constructed to reflect the design as it was in 1936. The Director's balcony, clock and the war memorial are all represented.

The loco shed has four roads, and is of kit construction. There is a coaling stage and a through route to the turntable. A loco railing line is laid behind the coaling stage connecting to the turntable.

Storage sidings

These give access to the loco depot, coaling stage, and provide storage for rolling stock.

Outdoors

The construction varies from the original metposts with plywood boards, to concrete blocks topped with plastic boards all covered with roofing felt. All electrical cables are housed within plastic conduit at the side of the running boards to provide weather protection.

A parcels train takes the centre road through Reading.

GWR King Class No. 6010 King Charles I *heading the 'Cornish Riviera Express' as it climbs away from St Margaret's Junction.*

1. Paddington to St Margaret's Junction

The line is laid as double track up and down main. There is a third track in the section to facilitate empty coaching movements into and out of Paddington. These lines curve on a nine feet radius and are on a rising gradient of 1 in 70. The section also includes a six arch viaduct based on the Wharncliff Viaduct at Hanwell.

2. The circle

This facilitates continuous up and down double track running. The down main has a passing loop between Old Oak Bridge and St Margaret's Junction. This section features a bridge based upon the single span over the River Thames at Maidenhead.

3. The reversing loop

A single line loop from the down main to the up main enables return running into Paddington.

4. Tunnel

Impressions of Box tunnel mouths are included at each end of a 6ft tunnel.

5. Reading Station

This is an impression of the station layout, circa 1936, with the 1870s building and clock tower on the down platform; and an appropriate matching building on the up platform. Awnings extend for four feet from the buildings.

The station area is provided with a goods loop on the up side, with a storage

A mineral train on 'The Circle'.

St Margaret's Junction.

Overall view of Reading Station area.

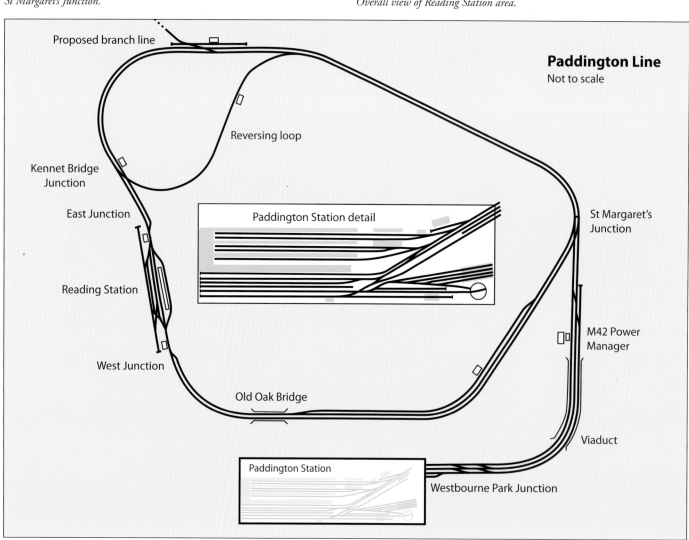

Paddington Line
Not to scale

Proposed branch line

Reversing loop

Kennet Bridge Junction

East Junction

Reading Station

West Junction

Old Oak Bridge

Paddington Station detail

St Margaret's Junction

M42 Power Manager

Viaduct

Westbourne Park Junction

Paddington Station

Awaiting departure from Reading.

siding on the west end, and a pilot siding and water tower at the east end. Signal boxes 'West Main Box' and 'East Main Box' are in situ, and the through lines include the third up line as appropriate. The station area is 40 x 3ft.

6. Branch line

A single branch line to the far corner of the garden is planned for the future. It will run to a typical Great Western branch line terminus to be housed in a 16 x 6ft shed.

Signals

The Paddington platforms are controlled by colour light signals as appropriate. There are other signals set out around the layout.

Lineside

Gradient posts are positioned where appropriate. Mile posts from Paddington at ¼ mile to 2 mile intervals are to be found around the layout in appropriate positions. There are five signal boxes around the layout in appropriate positions. There are a selection of platelayers and lamp huts required to run the layout.

Stock

Locomotives	23
Coaches	43
Other Rolling Stock	128

42XX Class tank loco No.4289 hauls a coal train through the countryside.

48XX Class 0-4-2T No.4839 leaves Reading with a short passenger train. This loco was renumbered in 1946 to 1439 when the class was changed to 14XX.

Reading station building and clock tower.

Bird's eye view of Paddington station.

Paddington loco shed with turntable to the rear.

Blackmore End *by Peter Lovell*

Photographs and description by the owner

There's now no end to Blackmore End

I said to my wife in 1999 "Do you think I could have a portable O gauge layout?" It was suggested that I should design it so it could be stored under the stairs, with a purpose-built fascia to hide it when not in use. It would also be capable of erection in less than 30 minutes, and dismantled and stored away in even less time.

Permission was granted and planning got underway. Paper templates for the track were made, and together with card shapes for rolling stock, a suitable layout was designed by crawling around on the lounge floor. Blackmore End – a small GWR branch terminus set in 1936 – was conceived, and a few months later the first train ran.

I had modelled in 4mm for more than 50 years, and at that time had a layout occupying a garage of some 23 x 9ft, using home built copper clad track. Operation was by conventional DC cab control with interlocked signals, and communication between operators was by bells and block instruments. Alex Jackson couplings were used with home produced electromagnets.

I decided to use the same methods of construction and operation for Blackmore End and, as I needed to save space, all turnouts were designed with a minimum radius of 5ft, and I have built all the track-work myself using copperclad sleepers and bullhead rail. This resulted in a scenic layout of 16ft, with a hidden 3-road sector plate serving two hidden kickback sidings. This fiddle yard arrangement enabled me to store five trains and access any one of them at will.

All this was stored under the stairs and, more importantly, could be transported to exhibitions in a Citroen Picasso leaving room for me and my assistant operator. The penultimate exhibition was at Guildex in 2003.

The 4mm layout in the garage had not been used for almost a year, so the decision was made to remove it, sell the stock, and give Blackmore End a

The Pannier on a local passenger arrival.

permanent home. The sector plate and kick back sidings were removed and replaced with a four foot radius curved track leading to a new junction station, Kimpton Road, on the other side of the garage. The platform buffers were also removed and a bridge was built under which the line would travel to a small fiddle yard with a four road traverser. There was now no end to Blackmore End, as it had become a through station.

Kimpton Road is a simple junction with a small goods yard, where trains can depart through either of two tunnels. The major route enters the new fiddle yard via a scissors crossover, having a simple entry turnout and 3 double slips enabling easy access to five storage roads and two kick-back sidings.

This situation prevailed until 2007. My wife and I found a double garage 18 x 18ft, with an additional 17 x 9ft workshop at the rear. We also liked the attached bungalow! The move was successfully made and the railway was soon

Romanies relaxing while the railway gets on with its business.

Overall view of the layout with Blackmore End on the right and Kimpton Road and fiddle yard on the left.

installed in its new home. Two years later, permission was also granted for an extension into the garage and another four foot radius curved track was laid to a new terminus, Chewton Magna.

I have always liked the idea that my trains should travel from one station to another, before disappearing to the world beyond. Operation of a layout in a prototypical fashion has always been a priority for me.

The current layout has five control panels, with switches for points, signals and isolating sections arranged on a mimic diagram of the track layout. Control is still by analogue cab control, with all signals with bounce, interlocked with the points, so if the signal is pulled off we know that the route has been correctly set.

GWR bell codes are used between signal boxes (ie control panels), together with a block instrument system. We will have an operating sequence eventually,

Control panel for Parkway and Underhill fiddle yard.

A 14XX Class tank loco and train wait in the bay platform at Blackmore End, pending the arrival of another local connection.

but at present trains are run as we fancy. Alex Jackson couplings are used with my own electro-magnets. These having about 3500 turns of 36swg enamelled copper wire, and are powered by 24 volt DC transformer. Therefore, we have completely hands off operation, and working on a 'receiver drives' basis the railway could be run in complete silence, as it is not necessary for operators to talk to each other.

A recent innovation has been the introduction of freight cards. Each wagon, van and horse box has its own laminated card. Each card has a picture of the vehicle together with a brief description. There is also a list of destinations down the right had side comprising of the three stations – each subdivided (e.g. bay platform, cattle dock, or by crane) on the left hand side, and the off stage fiddle yards. Each operating position has a row of boxes. These boxes include, for example, 'freight stock at Blackmore End' containing the relevant cards, 'next arrival,' 'freight ready to depart east bound' and 'freight ready to depart west bound.' Each operator has the responsibility to decide where his empty – or full – vehicles are to be sent. He puts a paper clip on the left hand side, against

that destination on the appropriate card, and puts all the cards for the next train into a clear plastic folder. He then places the folder into his 'freight ready for departure' box. He will soon offer the train to the signalman at the next station. After the two bells for 'train entering section' is acknowledged by the receiving operator, the despatching operator places the folder in the 'next arrival' box of the receiving operator. The receiving operator then carries out the instructions, and adds some of his full or empty stock, if he so desires, and so on ad nauseum. The system gives a purpose to shunting, especially when we have the golden rule – thou shall not shunt on the main line.

You may have realised by now that my interests do not include building locomotives or coaches, although I have built almost all of the goods vehicles. I have built most of the buildings either from scratch or by modifying suitable kits. Trees, laboriously made by unravelling cotton covered mains cable and twisting to shape, were rescued from the 4mm layout. I really enjoy building track and designing the associated electrical circuits needed to create a realistic scene through which my railway can be run in a prototypical fashion.

Kimpton Road arrival.

A distant view of the factory complex at Blackmore End.

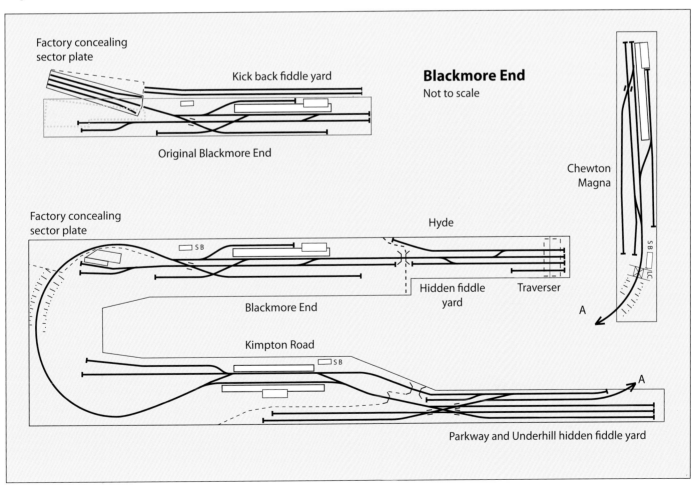

Tillynaught Junction *by Great North of Scotland Railway O Gauge Group*

Coastal Aberdeenshire prenationalisation

Photographs by David Thompson, description by Martin Cheshire

The model of Tillynaught Junction is as near to the prototype as modelling will allow. Built to scale 7mm/ft, the model was built over a 10 year period and represents this small and isolated junction on the Moray Coast Line, running between Elgin and Cairnie Junction and the branch line to Banff.

Looking from the viewing side, the main line from Elgin enters from the left, through the cutting and over a farm crossing to the station. Departing from the station and past the signal box, the line runs over the junction and under the road bridge to Carnie Junction, and Aberdeen, on the right. The station has three platforms, two serving the main line and, behind the station building, a third serving the branch to Banff. The magnificent station building was built by Jeff Weatherall, to whom we are extremely grateful. The remainder of the buildings have been built by the group and are faithfully reproduced from old photos supplied by many people.

Although the station buildings and signal box were demolished at closure, the Station Master's cottage to the left of the station building and the farm track underpass by the signal box remain today, as does the road bridge. The remainder of the site is overgrown and not distinguishable.

The operating period is from nationalisation of the railways to closure, and offers a large number of prototypical locomotives and stock representing many of the trains operating on the line during this period. Typically locomotives on the main line would normally have been shedded at Kittybrewster, and are LNER and British Railway standard types. The line to Banff has a number of pre-grouping locomotives that served on the branch over the operating period. A number of diesel locomotives are also used, representing the final years before closure.

Some trains have also been reproduced, with the through coaches to Aberdeen, hauled by B1 *Alexander Reith Gray,* fish trains to Buckie and Fiocherty, mixed goods trains with whisky for bottling and general goods, and the occasional pigeon and engineers trains. The branch is representative with short passenger and occasional mixed trains.

Tillynaught at its peak was a busy place, especially during the summer, with

Oil train passing through.

The signal box with a passenger train awaiting departure in the foreground.

A busy period of Tillynaught.

Ex-GNSR 0-4-4T Class G10 No.6892 shunts a goods arrival.

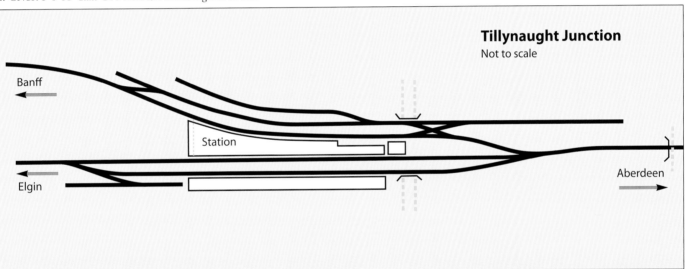

Tillynaught Junction
Not to scale

Banff

Station

Elgin

Aberdeen

Cattle wagon awaiting loading, with Scottish style B12 4-6-0 on the right. A number of these ex-GE locos were sent to Scotland by the LNER after grouping.

up to 30 scheduled passenger arrivals and departures a day. On Saturdays there were specials from nearby towns and cities taking people and Sunday school children for a day at the seaside at Banff.

Lastly, on the front of the layout there is a plaque in memory of Angus 'Gus' Cook a founder member of the group and an ex-railwayman, who sadly died during the models construction.

The 'Elgin' platform at Tillynaught.

Overall view of Tillynaught Junction.

A load of grey 'Fergies' passing through en route to Elgin.

View of the station area on the Banff side of the junction, with ex-GNSR tank loco 6892 on a short goods working.

Praa Sands *by Tony Collins*

Description and photos by the owner.

A space-saving layout for under £200

A very small through station on a GWR branch line, it's location, Praa Sands, actually sits on the west coast of the Lizard Peninsula, but never had a railway.

The layout consists of three baseboards giving a scenic length of 9ft 6in. This, plus cassette holders at each end, gives a total length of 14ft 6in, with a width of 12in.

The baseboards are made of 2 x 1in timber, with a track bed of ³/₈ in sundeala board. The backscene is thin plywood painted with satin emulsion and watercolours to depict a seascape based on Mounts Bay.

Track, points, buffers, signals and level crossing are by Peco, the last two items being considerably reduced in size as befits a minor branch line. The buildings are a mixture of Alphagraphics kits and scratch-built. The booking office, platform shelter and signal cabin are based, loosely, on GWR prototypes.

The arrivals and departures of trains are slightly masked by scenic breaks, being a copse at one end of the layout and a barn at the others.

Operating consists of some trains, goods or passenger, being shunted onto headshunt or siding. This allows passage of other trains passing through or stopping at the station. Wagons can be left on the siding for later collection after loading or unloading.

The total cost of this layout came to approximately £200 (at 2013 prices). There is a rudimentary but quite effective sound system courtesy of Peter Spoerer. This consists of a sound card and speaker under the layout.

A short mineral train arrives under Pannier power.

The local passenger train awaits the signal before departure.

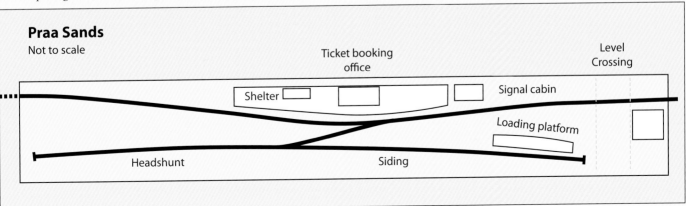

The mineral train waits at the loading platform.

The level crossing.

Local passenger train departs, whilst the schoolboys contemplate the Pannier shunting the mineral wagons.

The Pannier tank awaits the passage of the local before shunting its train.

Albion Quarry

Photos Courtesy Railway Modeller

Bob Alderman's Quarry Scene

Albion Quarry is located at the end of a now freight only branch off the ex-LNWR Bletchley-Oxford line. The branch has been curtailed from its original route of the LNWR which linked with the Great Central at Aylesbury. Now under the LMS it is showing some prosperity from the renewed working of Albion Quarry. The layout depicts the end of the line at a Portland stone quarry. The branch is fictitious, but the existence of Portland stone at this location is fact, but it was never quarried. The choice of subject reflects my interests; not only railways but local geology.

The quarry is undergoing a period of exceptional prosperity and has recently changed its haulage from horses to locomotives. It has been assumed that the quarry is owned by one of the Portland companies in Dorset. This allows the use of wagons based on the Merchants' Railway on Portland and other machinery from the Island.

The two lines shown, the quarry and branch are independent and only meet within the works.

The stone is extracted from the quarry and travels to the works where it is transferred to the branch vehicles. From here it goes worldwide.

The object of the layout is to illustrate the quarrying of dimension stone, which is stone intended for construction or elaborate mason's work. In this case it is Portland limestone. The limestone has joints between the blocks, cracks that occurred shortly after the lime sediment was laid down and was becoming the stone now being quarried. These are exploited to help remove the stone.

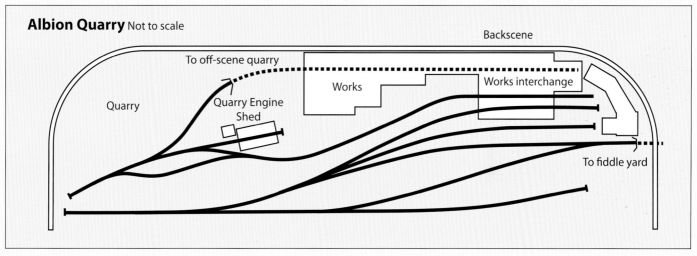

A view into the works. Two stone saws are visible at the back, one a circular saw, the other a reciprocating saw. These were modelled on examples in Purbeck quarry. Small overhead cranes are used to manouvre the stone blocks around the yard. At the front a mason is splitting a block with wedges and feathers.

They are also responsible for the stepped characteristics of the quarry.

The stone is transferred to the small wagons on the quarry line. These are based on horse-drawn examples of the Portland Merchants' Railway. The wagons are loaded and unloaded by scotch derricks. There is a steam-powered example in the quarry. The stone is lifted by the use of a quarry dog that grips the block as the weight is borne.

The works shows an example of an early circular saw; a later frame saw. There is a mason's yard were detail stone cutting is carried out.

Both finished work and stone blocks are transferred within the interchange shed for distribution to the wider world. Only the LSWR, later SR, had a special wagon for Portland stone traffic. There are a couple in SR liveries. Other railways relied on standard vehicles and loaded more lightly.

What actually happens in the transfer shed is that loaded wagons from the

The Ruston emerges from the lower quarry – off scene.

The Ruston with a load of stone destined for the works. The wagons are based on horse-drawn vehicles used on the Portland Merchants' Railway. In the background is the quarry loco shed with a Sentinel loco. There is fuel, oil and coal for the locos on a stage beside the water tower.

An Ivatt tank shunts the works – the left hand track is the quarry line. The large overhead crane transfers stone blocks and worked stone to mainline wagons.

The signal at the exit to the fiddle yard. Shunting requires locos to pass this signal at danger so there is a 'shunt ahead' board beside it.

quarry arrive; these are removed and substituted for empty ones. The empty wagons for the mainline have false floors with the stone attached and dropped in. These get emptied in the fiddle yard.

The fiddle yard is a double sector plate. It is long enough for a complete train plus a smaller sector plate for engine release or run around. To keep it within the envelope of the baseboard, they are all 4 x 3ft 6in, it folds for transport.

The layout is built on 9mm ply baseboards. Both completely covered and open top construction is used. The track of the branch is from C&L Components. The quarry line is Code 75 flat bottom rail spiked to ply sleepers. Both are to 32mm gauge. Tortoise motors operate the points.

As originally constructed the layout was wired for conventional DC control but has been modified to use DCC but it is not used.

The scenery has been constructed from card and overlain with newsprint

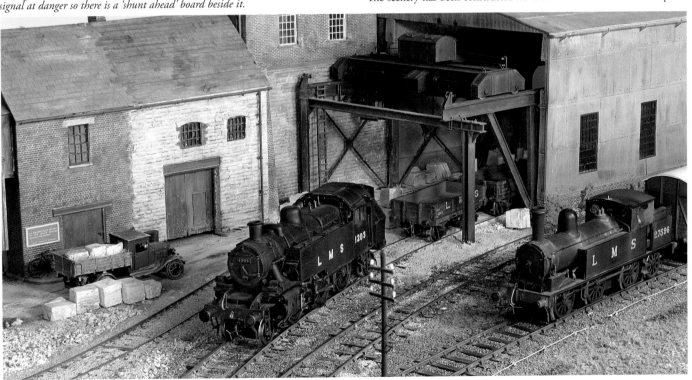

The Ivatt tank waits in the works sidings whilst the Coal Tank arrives on a trip to collect from or deliver to the works.

Another view of the Coal Tank preparing to run around and sort out the wagons for the works.

and finished with artex. It has been finished with artist's acrylic paints, Woodland Scenics and Heki fibre grass.

All the structures are scratch-built, mainly from plastikard.

Rolling stock is all kit built. The small quarry wagons are cast in white-metal from my own patterns (and are now part of the ABS range).

Two different coupling systems are used, Alex Jackson on the branch and HO scale Kadees in the quarry.

Another view into the quarry showing the crane with a stone block suspended. The block is held by 'quarry dogs', a scissor like arrangement that used the weight of the block to close them and hold it.

The Ivatt tank still waiting in the works whilst the Super D prepares to leave. This loco and the Coal Tank reflect the LNWR origins of the line.

Frecclesham *by Newport Model Railway Society*

Description by Steve Neill, photos by Craig Tiley courtesy Railway Modeller

Southern Railway branch among the North Downs

I personally believe railway clubs are about common friendships with aspects such as region, scale, gauge acting more as galvanising factors rather than the main driver. Our club is not alone in also not taking ourselves too seriously, a shared sense of humour being the most important attribute.

The previous O gauge layout, Hazelhurst, now decommissioned, stretched that sense of humour to the limit. At 42 x 3ft it required at least six able bodied members to load/unload and operate. That we struggled to cope became painfully obvious, plus as a large layout it did not generate the interest from show managers or public we had hoped for. When after the 2011 Bristol O gauge show, Hazelhurst was unloaded for the last time, by just two of us, the last vestiges of resistance to the idea of a new smaller/ lighter layout evaporated.

There were some pragmatic decisions made upfront regarding Frecclesham, which on this occasion we would mostly adhere to. Perhaps one of the most challenging was we'd try to generate a sense of space based on a simple track layout.

The model

In the past once the basic baseboards were built we would start laying track almost immediately, leaving presentation and lighting to a last minute panic before the first exhibition. We decided not to make this mistake again. The boards were from Model Railway Solution kits, customised for us to re-use existing legs. The layout also has a solid fascia which bolts to the layout in two pieces, joined at the top by the station name board. Whilst it took some discipline to resist starting on the layout, finishing these was worth it. Creating the 'letter box' presentation often seen in smaller scales was I think one of our better decisions!

The trackwork (Quart into a pint pot)

A scenic section at 14 x 3ft is not generous in 7mm scale. So having the simple track diagram in mind, members Tony Bennett and Rod Hall worked on fitting it into the space available. A key design goal was to enable the 3-coach birdcage set we had available to be operated with a run around. They came up with the gracefully curved scheme we have today, which would include for the station throat a 3-way point, double slip and an outside slip. This

Frecclesham signal box built from a Churchward Models kit.

H Class 31533 prior to departure with a local passenger train.

Superpower – Battle of Britain Class No.34056 Croydon *departs on a two coach local train.*

C Class 31723 arrives with a short goods.

arrangement saved over 2ft compared to using Peco points.

In parallel with the carpentry activity, Tony proceeded to build the point work to 31.2mm track standards using the Brookesmith (ply and rivet) technique. Unfortunately whilst Tony was to see his track laid on the baseboards and some initial test running he lost his battle with illness and passed away in the Autumn of 2012. His 10 year old grandson would later join us at the first show at which the completed Frecclesham was exhibited.

Signalling

So while we were not taking things too seriously, we did want to get our fiction right. So the track plan was duly given to a professional signalman and a signal diagram returned. For a number of us signalling is a bit of a dark area, so there was a little surprise that such a simple track plan generated so many signals. All signals are working (servo operated) and during a show after a little acclimatisation we now tend to actually drive to them, even ground signals.

Maunsell N Class 2-6-0 in the station loop.

Rush hour at Frecclesham.

Scenery

There is a clear tension with having a relatively small space and yet wanting to achieve a sense of space, which was one of our key goals. So in the course of the development features were ditched and we settled on a less is more approach. This meant we lost a narrow gauge line, Banisters Mini-Bakery, a road bridge and Grip Tight Tyres Garage. At the time we were a little sad to see the narrow gauge line go, but it was the right collective decision.

How to hide the entrance to the layout? Wanting to try something different to a bridge or tunnel the final approach was to obscure the entrance with a raised front section representing the end of a cutting. A barn would add interest and provide a solid visual barrier. Then with trees strategically positioned and configured to obscure the entrance stock would appear thru the foliage into view.

This is where I got a little carried away becoming addicted to making trees.

Schools Class 30915 Brighton *leaves Frecclesham with a local passenger train.*

M Class No.30055 arrives at the main platform with a push-pull service. Built from a Martin Finney kit the loco was painted by Ian Rathbone.

They are built using the twisted wire approach – there are plenty of articles and books that cover this. I used TreeMendous kits and their products, indeed their bark powder was used extensively as ground cover. Drying as it does to a grey colour it is not prone to showing white. The two raised areas were built off layout at home and then planted into position. Here we got lucky, as you can see in some of the pictures the trees almost meet up over the running in line.

After the first outing as a work in progress it became quite apparent that the fiddle yard end of the layout was dominating the overall picture simply due to the sheer number of trees at that end. So rather than thin the trees out more

were made for the station end. There are still spaces I have my eye on for future cultivation.

Buildings

Trawling through our books for suitable station buildings we came across Westerham, with it's simple wooden constructed structures. The station buildings have been well documented so getting drawings proved very straightforward, and there is an excellent book on the line. I guess I've let the cat out of the bag and revealed Frecclesham is a fictional location.

D1 Class 4-4-0 No.31505 is poised to depart the main platform with a passenger service following the arrival of C Class No.31723 on a goods. Both locos were built from David Andrews kits.

The goods shed is based on the example that existed at Westerham. It was scratch-built from strip wood by club member Rob Foot.

At the club one evening, armed with pictures and drawings of the station building and goods shed, we quickly decided they were suitable prototypes, being simple and attractive. At this point Rob Foot quickly put his hand up and announced "I'll build them, I've always wanted to have a go at 7mm buildings." Volunteers are worth 10 pressed men. What seemed like just a few weeks later he arrived with the finished station building, or so we thought? Wrong, the model we were admiring was only a mock-up. This mock-up has so far been to six shows, receiving favourable comments at all. At the Carmarthen show Rob was especially pleased when another exhibitor recognised the building.

The goods shed is also by Rob's hand, made from strip wood. This structure looked particularly lonely when first exhibited, so now has a tree for company.

Westerham had the foundations for a demolished engine shed with pit filled in – this was also re-created although not slavishly. This has drawn a number of questions at shows so far, clearly it has intrigued a few people. The water tank was a quite impressive affair for such a small station, but was probably part of the future expansion plans. The water tank should really have been next to this old engine shed foundations, but the station end was still looking sparse so it was located based on visual impact.

Operation

Had Frecclesham existed it is the sort of location that would have seen a light service, at best an hourly pull-push service. Clearly this is not enough to sustain interest, so we operate a much more diverse sequence and stock.

The name

If you are still at all curious, the name is a concoction of Eccles and Friars Balsam, with 'ham' added at the end giving Frecclesham.

Final thoughts

This has been an interesting exercise, and quite eye opening. The constraints that a small layout brings to the table are as liberating as they are challenging. Liberating in the sense that once one faces the fact not everything will fit, one tends to focus on the key elements.

Appendix

Whenever one reads about a layout in the modelling press there is often a background history for the location, here's ours...

Brief history of Frecclesham

As with many small market towns Frecclesham craved a railway connection to London and the coast. There was a belief that railways would bring prosperity, and towards the end of the great railway expansion of the 19th century an Act of Parliament was approved in 1871 to build the line from Lower Bannister through to Hazelhurst with a station at Frecclesham.

In the end the line only reached as far as Frecclesham. This was due to a combination of financial mis-management by the then MD (Major B.Nock, survivor of Balaclava) and the woefully incompetent surveyor (Mr H.Crun) who actually built the line from Upper Bannister.

The line finally opened in 1901, successfully missing the golden age of railway building and any chance of deriving financial benefit. Always a sleepy backwater it retained pretensions of connecting through to Hazelhurst. Hence the general layout is that of a through station rather than a terminus. Frecclesham marketed itself as The Home of the Alternative Eccles Cake, a delicacy which was unique to the area. To the unwary this could come as a shock, containing as it did potted shrimps in the place of raisins. It was access to shrimps from the coast that was the motivation behind early attempts to establish a rail link.

The rail link came too late to save the pungent delicacy disappearing from the dinner tables of the nation, a situation few lamented.

Local historical figures

Major B. Nock (1820 to 1905) : Local opinion was divided on the Major, he portrayed himself as a man of independent means and a survivor of the Battle of Balaclava claiming to have taken part in the Charge of the Light Brigade. His detractors suggested his survival was due to oversleeping that fateful morning. He was a significant figure in the early history of the railway, becoming MD of the company. Resigned his post after accounting irregularities were uncovered, nothing was ever proven.

H.Crun (1795 – 1892) : His early life is shrouded in some mystery, earliest records reveal him as batman to Lord Raglan during the Crimean Campaign, by which time Henry was already in his 60s. His army career was cut short after the inadvertent substitution of a dry cleaning ticket for Light Brigade orders caused some embarrassment to his employer.

Netherwood Sidings *by Graham Clarke*

Photos and description by the owner.

The Woodhead route in the 1960s

Introduction

Netherwood sidings started out as a test track consisting of a single track oval with a 4-road fiddle yard on one side, and a double track loop on the other. The non-fiddle yard side of the layout provided the scope for scenic development but it took me some time to settle on what to build. I finally decided on a Woodhead Route layout as I had been involved in a 4mm club project based on this line.

Planning

The concept is a small yard to the east of Sheffield where coal trains arrive from local collieries and are coupled into longer rakes to be taken over the Woodhead line by electric locos. The trains from the local collieries are, of course, diesel hauled and operate as half trains as the collieries have limited siding space. This is what happened in reality at Wath, but I have based the layout on Rotherwood rather than Wath as there were no passenger trains at Wath.

The fact that the test track had a double track on that side meant that the scenic area could be double track and so the track plan was based on a double junction, similar to the one at Wath. I added a headshunt for the yard and then arranged four sidings the full length of the yard. These disappear beneath a road bridge giving the impression that the yard is much longer. There are also a

The allotment holders take a breather, while the railway continues to run its daily schedule.

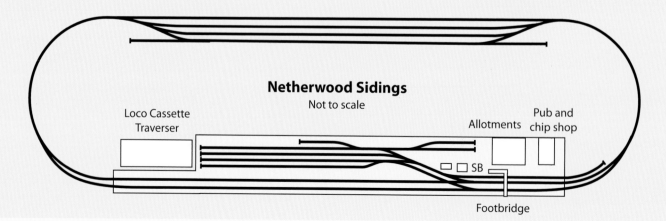

Netherwood Sidings

Not to scale

Loco Cassette Traverser

Allotments

Pub and chip shop

SB

Footbridge

Diesel and electric power pass on the main lines.

The pub and chip shop with a fine view over the railway.

couple of loco holding sidings and a short brake van siding which can also house the 08 that shunts the yard.

To give more fiddle yard capacity at exhibitions, I added a couple of extra exhibition only scenic boards at the front and corresponding boards in the middle of the fiddle yard.

Construction

The layout is normally housed in the loft and so the boards had to be light. I used 6mm and 9mm birch ply for their construction. Each scenic board has a ladder beam on each long side. These were made from 100mm wide strips of 6mm ply with softwood spacers in between. This arrangement makes it possible to have a pocket at each corner into which legs can be plugged. The curved end boards and fiddle yard boards were made from 6mm ply and the sides project above track level to provide a barrier for any derailed stock.

Track is mainly Peco with bullhead for the hidden trackage and flat bottom on the main lines at the front. The points in the hidden area were made from Peco bullhead rail on fibreglass PCB sleeper strip. The points on the visible part of the main line were built from Peco individulay components on a plan reduced to scale from a BR standard drawing. The points in the yard were built from Peco chairs and rail with plywood sleepers. All the points are operated by Tortoise motors.

Scenery construction made much use of expanded polystyrene and foam board to keep the weight down. Buildings are removable and made from foam board covered with scribed filler or from plastikard. The permanent way hut is a commercial item.

The overhead line equipment was built from various brass sections soldered together. The wire is 28SWG nickel silver. The wire is not energised and stops at the end of the scenic section. When installed in the loft there is insufficient clearance for the pantographs on the hidden section and for this reason all the locos are fitted with servos to raise and lower the pantographs.

Operation

The layout is controlled by a MERG DCC system with hand held controllers on wander leads.

The layout is operated as two groups of services. One group is made up of trains that do not use the yard and just run round the layout from one end of the fiddle yard to the other. A train leaves each end of the fiddle yard at the same time running in opposite directions. They pass on the double track at the front.

The other group of trains are coal trains, empty and loaded, which operate in and out of the yard. The locos for these are stabled in the sidings behind the signal box.

Double-headed power for the empties returning to base.

Bay Ridge Harbor Rail Road *by Neville Rossiter*

A 1950s inspired American layout

Photos and description by the owner.

The inspiration for Bay Ridge Harbor Rail Road (BRHRR) came from the images of the New York Harbor in the 50s, and is a permanent layout in a 27 x 27ft room in the owner's house in Perth, Western Australia. It has taken 25 years to get to the current stage and there are still more details to be added. It gives Neville and two friends much pleasure to operate weekly.

The layout is 1/48 O scale using Peco and Marcway track, all electrically controlled from control panels. Being an industrial railroad there is no passenger service only freight. Way bills are used for each car and the BRHRR has an operating sequence of approximately 5 hours which is very flexible.

Everything on the BRHRR has been built by Neville except the electrical wiring which his good friend Bruce Temperley has finished to a very high standard. It is DC controlled throughout using Morley controllers from England.

I am not frightened to try new ideas and the layout has, apart from the usual freight sidings, a large US Army military base with the appropriate sidings and rolling stock.

There is a staging yard at one end of the layout that represents the rest of the world where all trains are received and despatched to Bay Ridge Yard. They are then made into the appropriate trains for each district.

All locomotives are Atlas O Diesels and the freight cars a mixture of Atlas, Lionel Scale, Intermountain, MTH Scale, Red Caboose, and Weaver freight cars.

All rolling stock including locomotives are fitted with scale metal wheels and Kadee couplers for reliability. Everything apart from the track and bench work comes from America.

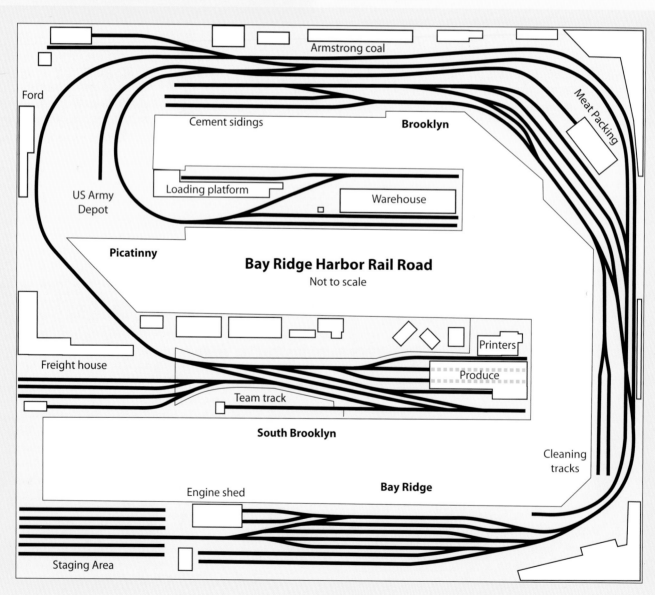

The meat packing area and cattle reception pens.

The military area of the layout.

Boxcars awaiting loading.

General view of Brooklyn loading area.

Another view of the meat packing area.

Aerial view of South Brooklyn.

Winsham Junction *by Jeff Rodway and Barry Sumsion.*

Description and photographs by Barry Sumsion

Or a little of what you fantasy does you good!

Winsham Junction is the O gauge layout built in the loft area of Jeff Rodway's bungalow by Jeff and myself. It started about fifteen years ago when Jeff moved into his present home and found a loft area prepared for intended upstairs bedrooms, being approached by a proper staircase, fully floored and with supporting uprights about fifteen feet apart. Jeff's wife had ideas about storage but we had decidedly different ideas. We had both recently been involved with 5 inch and 7¼ inch gauge live steam but as our knees got older so the locos got heavier. With an area measuring approximately 48 feet by 20 feet overall, O gauge beckoned. The twenty first century approached and so we thought that the then comparatively new digital control, DCC, was the way to go.

So what to build and where? We both are fans of the Southern Region of British Railways, although as was to be proved in time, if it involved models of steam engines, then it became quite a mixture. I researched areas of the West Country that might involve the Southern, the Great Western and the Somerset & Dorset. I discovered that there had been various attempts by the people of Bridgwater to build a railway linking their port on the Bristol Channel with the English Channel. It never happened – but what if? And here is where we invoke a dose of fantasy tinted a little by what might just have happened. On the S&D line from Evercreech Junction to Highbridge is the village of Edington from where the Bridgwater Railway branched off to its small terminus in Bridgwater. Ah but the line was, of course, upgraded and Bridgwater became a through station with the line extending south and slightly eastwards towards the south coast of England. Winsham is a village on the southern border of Somerset with Dorset where to this day the old LSWR line to Exeter passes through although today it is only a single track main line. Entering from the north west comes the S&D line with its station to the north of the village. It crossed the LSWR a little to the east of Winsham on its way through the Dorset hills via Beaminster to a terminus and the port at Bridport. The LSWR with the Midland were responsible for the running of the S&D and built an incline to create a junction between the two lines. Hence Winsham Junction. Meanwhile the Great Western also wishing to reach the south coast extended from their station at Chard but the LSWR were having none of it, and the GW line ended at Winsham Junction. From Winsham the GW cut their losses and extended eastwards to their station at Yeovil via Crewkerne which station was in the centre of the town, unlike the LSWR one which is well out of town to the south. So what does all this fantasy give us? Well four continuous running lines all with storage roads. There are the main SR up and down lines London to Exeter, the GW line from Chard continuing to Yeovil and on the high level the S&D on its way from Bridgwater to Bridport.

That's the raison d'etre for our railway and it is designed so that running can take place independently on the four main circuits as well as being able to move between any of the circuits in any direction. This is made easier by the adoption of DCC. The layout was properly drawn up and WAS planned. However changes have been made as it has evolved and we now have, or are developing, a main shed, Hewish, a small GW servicing shed and a round-house style area for the growing collection of heritage models (pre-group and pre-nationalisation. The heritage collection resident, but not all belonging to Jeff or me, has necessitated the creation of a bank of sidings known as the museum sidings. The main station does have platforms and a main building built from Townstreet parts by Steve Neill and the S&D station is formed from an end-to-end layout we acquired at an exhibition but is now a through station, and definitely in need of some TLC. That means that running is the main activity and we really do intend one day to create a credible scenery for the trains to

Southern Railway Class S15 30846 on a London bound milk tram.

run through. We've bought the ballast! For the main layout we try to model the period between 1954 and 1959. That gives us, in many instances, models of engines that we remember from our youth. A list of the locos and rolling stock would be a little boring but suffice it to say that a choice of about 50 locos is not unusual and with few exceptions they are all good runners and many are fitted with authentic sound systems. The layout is frequently used by the producer of arguably the best of British sound systems. as a testing ground.

Although the layout is far from finished frequent visitors, many of them Guild members come to watch and play trains, drink tea and eat cakes! With the intensive running we achieve, continuous maintenance is required and if we have a problem then we put it right. We always say don't blame the loco or the track – put it right.

I don't currently have the appropriate software to draw up the track plan but I hope the photographs will give some idea of what we have.

Another view of the milk tram.

A Spamcan takes the 'Devon Belle' through the junction.

Heyside *by Richard Lambert*

Photographs courtesy of Railway Modeller

A Lancashire & Yorkshire Railway 7mm scale layout in BR days

Heyside is a real location although a station was never built there. It is situated north east of Manchester between the former stations of Royton Junction and Shaw and Crompton on the route between Manchester Victoria and Rochdale via Oldham.

The layout has some fine urban and industrial buildings and they present a most imposing backdrop. Inspiration has been taken from the books by Jeffrey Wells on the Oldham Loop and structures from Werneth, Shaw and Royton can be seen.

To the left of the station is a goods yard with a goods loop constructed just beyond the platform end. This yard has an end loading dock and the area between the main sidings has been laid with setts and longitudinal sleepers adjacent to the rails in typical L&Y fashion.

The huge goods warehouse is modelled on the structure located at Royton Junction. To the left of it are two rows of worker cottages. These are typical of the area and have been located on either side of the main line cutting, inspired by the east end of Glodwick Road station, adding more height to the layout. A

road bridge and footbridge mask the inevitable scenic break with the line plunging into twin single bore tunnels modelled on Farnworth east portal.

The station buildings and platforms are typical L&Y, as are the lattice footbridges to the platforms on which two signals are sited as at Werneth. The parachute tank is off the end of the platform to provide improved sighting of the signal gantry.

To the right of the station a coal yard and factory siding with loading ramp has been built. A small loco servicing point has been incorporated modelled on the facility at Oldham Werneth. The rail over rail bridge has been modelled on that at the top of Hunt's Bank Incline, 1½ miles from Victoria Station.

It is often difficult to properly locate signals, so the assistance of a Network Rail signaller was obtained to ensure realistic signals and movements. The main line has a mixture of L&Y and LMS signals with the L&Y structures modified

The gardeners stop work for a chat with the crew of Jubilee No.45642 Boscowen.

to upper quadrant operation. The gantry at the coal yard end of the layout, modelled on that at Victoria East Junction signal box is built in wood just like its prototype and features signals for both directions plus a calling on arm to facilitate shunting. In the goods yard are examples of L&Y lower quadrant signals, each one being faithfully modelled from examples illustrated in the Jeffery Wells' books, and in The Lancashire and Yorksire Railway Society book on signalling.

Operation

The layout has a double track main line plus branch line with trains stored in hidden sidings, five loops for each main line plus five sidings for the branch line. DCC control is used with a number of sound equipped locomotives. The period modelled is the late 1950s into the 60s, steam and diesel locomotives plus diesel multiple units can be seen in operation. All the pointwork has been constructed to 31.5mm gauge and each point has been hand built to fit its location. The minimum radius is 6ft although on the branch one curve is slightly below this standard.

The station has a regular stopping service from and to Manchester, and these trains are presumed to run to Rochdale, Bury, Bolton as well as circle trains to Manchester Victoria via Castleton. There are a number of semi fast services which do not stop at the station. These trains are for destinations such as Southport via Bolton and Wigan, Blackpool via Bolton and Preston as well as to destinations across the Pennines. The branch line enjoys a frequent connecting service with trains operated largely by push and pull fitted locos and coaches although diesel multiple units are also known to turn up on some occasions.

In keeping with the industrial nature of the area freight trains are a major feature. L&Y survivors can be seen shunting and handling some lighter trains. Heavier trains are hauled by the larger steam and diesel locomotives.

Every effort has been made to run only locomotives and stock appropriate to the line, with duplication of loco types evident. Again the Jeffery Wells books have been the guide. Most locomotives have been weathered to varying degrees but given the proximity of the area to Crewe and Horwich works the occasional ex-works machine can be seen.

LMS 4-4-0 Class 2P No.40671 arrives with a local passenger working.

BR Class 9F No.92006 passes through Heyside, whilst Fairburn 2-6-4T No.42091 stops with a local passenger train.

A very dirty 'Mucky Duck' Ivatt Class 4MT No.43152 on a through mineral train.

Ex-L&Y 2-4-2T No.50757 in lined BR livery passes by.

Haytor Vale *by Fred Walton*

Photographs by Dreek Shore courtesy of Railway Modeller

A typical GWR country branch terminus

This layout ticks all the boxes for a layout described in the heading. Two photographs of my layout are taken by Derek Shore. They show both ends of the layout and signals. 4808 in the main platform awaiting instruction to move forward to shunt within the layout. Above the dustbin on the left are banner repeater discs as there is a line of sight problem to observe the signal arms adjacent to the signal box. The impressive station sign tells it all.

Larger locos are rare at Haytor Vale, but the Director's Saloon arrives with 7800 *Torquay Manor* in charge. This loco has the original larger chimney as when built, and the full passenger livery of the 1930s. This view is the end of the layout toward the cassette arrangement beyond the bridge. To the left is the coal dock and on the right the refuge siding. Note the vehicle on the bridge of a well known West Country company. The signal bracket is protected by two banner repeaters the other side of the bridge. Note the shunt ahead ground signal next to the advanced starter when leaving the scene, and a larger water tank which straddles the siding at the buffer stops.

If anyone is contemplating O gauge in a limited space, the following criteria should be considered for interest and prototypical operation. This could apply to a terminus or end to end arrangement.

- A large number of loco and stock movements gives increased operational interest.
- With a terminus, the presence of a siding where the arriving train can be

An interloper from the Southern Railway, an Adams 0-4-2T, arrives at Haytor Vale.

The signal box in the early evening.

7800 Cookham Manor *arrives with the Directors Saloon.*

48XX Class 0-4-2T No.4808 on shunting duties.

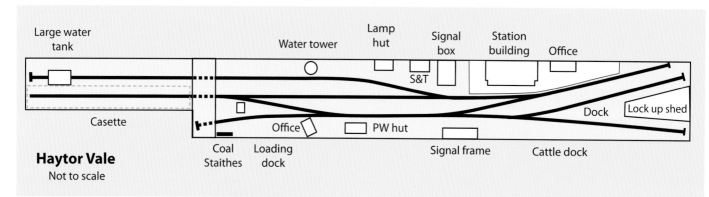

Haytor Vale
Not to scale

Large water tank — Casette — Coal Staithes — Loading dock — Office — Water tower — Lamp hut — S&T — PW hut — Signal box — Signal frame — Station building — Office — Cattle dock — Dock — Lock up shed

An active time at the loading dock.

The presence of working signals is also a pleasure during a running session. Haytor Vale is a complete working example of the above, enhanced by its buildings and atmospheric railway operation. Enough to inspire?

held, as opposed to having to depart the scene immediately also adds interest to the layout.
- If the loco run round is in the central area it can be better seen by viewers
- Sidings left and right of centre provide train movements along the length of the layout.

Haytor Vale has all the above in the track plan. Note also that the goods shed is on a dock platform, which does not obscure wagons.

Heavy work at the loading dock for the local coal merchant.

Hedingham *by Alan Turner helped by Geoff Byman*

An artistic impression of 1930s Lincolnshire

No doubt I could have, or might have, made other things than model railways, for it is the nature of many humans to want to create, for a variety of reasons.

W J Bassett-Lowke said: "The desire to make things is without doubt and is common to all humanity. From the earliest recorded times, man has endeavoured to reproduce objects in miniature."

I am sure that many of us think about the past, especially in later life. Not that those days were necessarily better, but judging by the number of television programmes dealing with the past, one can assume that a great number of people have an interest and feeling for what has gone before. We tend to remember, in most cases, the imagined golden days of childhood and youth. I certainly do, even though some of those years were during the Second World War.

My father was a signalman on the London and North Eastern Railway, and I was born at a station on the East Lincolnshire line. The sights, sounds and smells of the railway were there for me, day and night. With my father, the friendly staff and the local coal merchant, no part of the station and yard remained unexplored. My daily diet ranged from ex-GN Atlantics to humble C12s.

We moved to a situation on the East Coast Main Line during the war and the best of the LNER locomotives were seen, though not in the condition depicted in my pre-war books and postcards. I have a photographic memory and so many images of those years remain.

Still during the war, we moved to the huge junction of Barnetby, and now former Great Central locomotives were the norm. So my childhood was fed on a rich diet of LNER experiences, with a sneaking admiration for certain crimson LMS locomotives. I dreamt of nothing more than to eventually work on the footplate, though fully aware of the reality of the hard, dirty work and unsocial hours.

Gaining a scholarship to the local grammar school botched that, as it was drummed into me that a career away from the railway was my future.

I had, from a young age, made things, and as a student in the 1950s I became inspired by such people as Ahern, Denny, Ilife Stokes and others, familiar to older readers. I still have my first copy of *Railway Modeller* from August 1952, priced 1/6d. With very limited resources, everything had to be done on the cheap or preferably at no cost. My main interest was making models of interesting old buildings, which I enjoyed drawing. Railways featured in these non-working dioramas. Eventually small working models were made. In due

The view of a well populated engine shed early on a summer morning.

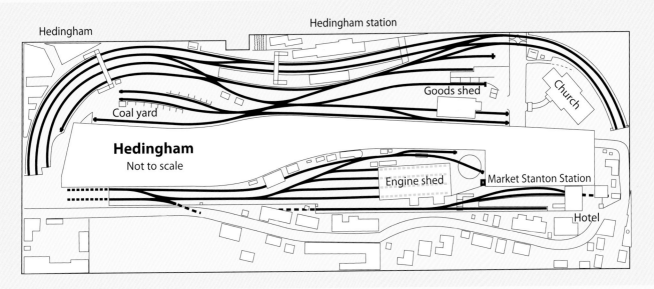

The staff deep in conversation. Railway matters or the weekend football results?

course followed a normal lifetime of work, marriage and housebuilding, and life passed.

When my wife died, interest was totally lost, and 40 or so years of modelling was disposed of. A move was made, and purely by chance the new dwelling happened to have bedrooms in a row. This indicated to those close to me that there was potential for space to start modelling again, as a very necessary therapeutic creative activity. The foregoing thoughts will indicate the reasons for my style of modelling, as well as the choice of period and company.

I had always admired 7mm models and felt that this was the smallest scale that gave a feeling of mass. However I had never seriously considered modelling in O gauge, imaging that cost and space put this size well out of my reach. Years ago, I had met and kept in touch with the late Jack Ray of O gauge fame, and consequently visited the nearby, large layout of his friend, the late Arthur Dewar. I was much impressed, but at the time still dismissed the idea of O gauge for me. My only personal experience of 7mm scale was my building a small museum diorama, and later a North Staffordshire Railway diorama for my friend, the late Dr Chadwick.

I was now persuaded that if I knocked some walls down I could create a modest 7mm model. This apparently was for my wellbeing.

Baseboards were built round the space in the usual way, and stupidly a very quick start was made, without serious planning. At that stage, I did not know what I really wanted, other than that the layout would be for continuous running, to watch trains passing by. There would also be storage loops for any future acquisitions. Initially I had a C12 tank, built as a return favour, and a few wagons from a static diorama, but no serious plans.

Time being of the essence, it was easy to buy mainly Peco track, whilst various points, including scratch-built, were considered adequate for my then needs. Cork tiles were used as underlay. Continuous alterations and developments took place, with various features, structures and buildings taking precedence over rolling stock. There was no long-term planning just on the hoof changes made if something proved unsatisfactory, or new ideas cropped up. The one constant was the idea to have a railway in a landscape, an impression, a three dimensional picture that was to be looked at, as much as operated.

The period modelled remained in the late 1930s, when I was becoming aware

The typical GN somersault signal gives the 'right away' to the local passenger train.

The coal yard at Hedingham.

The chapel and adjacent cottage.

of my railway environment. At that time there was plenty of pre-grouping rolling stock on the cash strapped LNER, the livery on company wagons was being simplified, and the colour scheme on structures gradually being changed. It was familiarity. Had I realised then just how much rolling stock was going to be scratch-built and acquired, I could perhaps have chosen a late pre-grouping period. However, in my period there was still much of interest, when towns and villages still had many old buildings, shops, street furniture and horse drawn vehicles. So it was a case of modelling that which I clearly remembered from childhood.

At one stage, the whole layout became far too complicated, with two levels, the former GNR on the higher level and the former GCR on the lower, with a far too steeply sloped connection. Signals and structures indicated former ownership. Rationalisation had to take place.

One everlasting feature has been the hidden storage loops, now under removable scenic sections.

The increasing need for more space led to the building of an extension, giving another ten feet. Of course 30 x 12ft may seen generous to those without such space, but there is never enough. It was fortunate that I chose to build an extension rather than go into yet another bedroom. Visits by my son and his family cause slight accommodation problems as it is.

Friends, led by David Hubbard, who seeing the potential had also changed to O gauge, altered the wiring and controls as necessary, and everyone contributed ideas. Some had skills which filled the gaps in my repertoire. Apart from locomotives, it is a case of I build and others make things work.

My railway has been finished for some years. The final layout has a modest station on a supposed secondary line, a decent goods yard and a junction for a minor branch.

The locomotive shed and yard just happened to be near the station because of space, and is basically to store and display locomotives. Construction of the building extension meant a bit of protruding wall, round which the railways had to curve, but this, together with bridges and structures, make trains seem longer than they really are.

The main station sees the usual through and stopping trains, with branch connections. The latter gave me the excuse to build older stock, cascaded down

to minor lines. At one stage I had a quite spacious branch station, but this had to go when the engine shed was built.

I was left with some interesting branch stock which I rather liked. A simpler branch was built, with just a run round and bay, but with an interesting overhead station building, under which the line would appear to continue. There are now four hidden branch storage roads, in which trains can be held, between Hedingham and Market Stainton.

The engine shed and yard was suggested by friends, so that the growing collection of locomotives could be displayed and opportunities for more activity provided.

Three or four people can now be occupied, though I prefer only three at a time, for practical reasons.

The main lines, the goods yard, the branch and shed can all be operated independently. Obviously they interact for shunting, branch exchange, engine changing, running round and so on.

There are some very difficult and thought-provoking moments at times. My grandsons are proving masters of operating and have super memories for all aspects, no doubt enhanced by computer game experience.

DCC would enhance everything, and would be a way forward, but not for me, due to the linked factors of age, time, cost and disruption. Simply put, it is too late for me.

The whole railway represents a former GNR line, made obvious by buildings and signalling. Hedingham building was inspired by some of the stations between Lincoln and Honington. The name was chosen merely because I enjoyed a book called *Hedingham Harvest*, recording life in a small Lincolnshire community in the late 19th century. The goods yard and shed offer facilities for most types of local traffic, whilst the back road is used by all branch trains, as a lay-by and for shunting, when available.

The cattle dock is a rail and road type, replacing the earlier wooden type, as at Burgh-le-Marsh. A pump has replaced the old well.

There is no timetable or even sequence, the operators just running trains as they wish and co-operating.

The connection from the engine shed to the main layout is by a hidden junction on the branch route.

The talking continues.

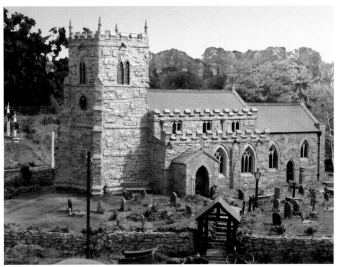

Headingham Church. The railway line passes close by to the rear.

The environs of the engine shed.

I have too many engines, now forming a collection, and most are kit built. Although the majority are of ex GCR and GNR types, there are later LNER representatives and visitors from the M&GN, GER and LMS.

I am not in the ready to run price bracket, but have several, obtained in return for buildings and other works. Larger locomotives do not usually appear on shed, as they would look totally out of place at this modest establishment.

All engines are well run in and are therefore good, reliable runners. Selwyn, our loco man, soon sorts out any rare faults.

It is useful for operators to become familiar with different locomotives, for, like the real things, they have various characteristics. Some have flywheels, some extra pick ups and recent examples have the American style of pick up.

We have not felt the need for compensation. The heaviest good trains are hauled by such power as the 02 or 04, whilst the J6, J11 and the many 4-6-0s seem good for anything. There are favourites for certain trains, such as the V2 on the express parcels, and the K3 on the perishables. The latter brings back memories of the K3s, rocking and rolling west from Grimsby and spraying fish smelling water from the melting ice.

My pleasure is observing trains from a rail-level viewpoint, whilst friends operate. An M&GN Class C on a visiting racehorse special, a D2 on vintage stock for the engineer or the lovely crimson Patriot or Compound on a LMS excursion provide extra interest. The latter carries an inspector.

I have had a go at the loco building, but have not found this interesting enough to continue. Each to his own. We all have our preferences, as with operating where one might prefer the branch or shed, whilst someone else prepares shunting the yard. Obviously there is interaction and co-operation due to conflicting moves and so on, as in real life.

Most engines were chosen because I actually saw them (or, most probably, saw them), as they passed my home, or they were observed on journeys. I still have an exercise book titled *Scripture* from 1948, but filled with engine observations. Wagons and coaches are a different matter, and I have scratch-built about 75 per cent, using 1mm ply, artists mounting board and plastic card. Long gone are the days when I would flatten out toothpaste tubes when they were thin metal, and prick through with a pin to suggest bolt in the wagon strapping. In these days of plastic rodding it is so easy to put on individual bolts

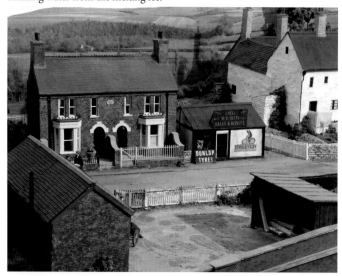

The tyre shop awaiting customers? Or maybe it's a quiet Sunday morning.

Top-up time at the garage.

Class N5 0-6-2T No.5903 awaits the signal prior to departure on a local passenger train. This class of loco is ex-GCR and built when Mr H Pollitt was the CME.

and rivets. I must emphasise that I am not a rivet counter, merely an impressionist. I have nothing against coach and wagon kits, except the cost and the fact that I have wanted items that are not available. Any materials are used that are suitable for a particular job. The gas tank wagon, for example, is made up using lengths cut from a broom handle of the right diameter.

Perhaps I have too many private owner wagons, but I had an interest in those from my area, as well as those that would have passed through.

As others have done more recently, I made personal examples for friends.

The railway is fully signalled. For interest, I have made a variety, ranging from pure GNR, to GNR with LNER additions and changes, to pure LNER. Some are concrete and others are wood and concrete with metal brackets. The only kits used were a couple of metal lattice types, to save time. Having at one time owned a number of full size original signals, helped the modelling.

All buildings are made from scratch, using artists mounting board, clad with embossed bricks or other suitable material such as plaster.

All buildings have been inspired by originals, though in some cases using only the frontages and fictitious names. Models of actual buildings seem much more realistic to me, rather than fictional examples. As a student I had a fondness for old buildings, and I wish I still had the drawings I made in the 1950s. I have made use of photographs in the very plentiful books on villages and towns. These can give so much information, ranging from the harness on

a horse passing with a cart, to the position of a village pump. There are additions I could make to my model, such as a threshing set or a road mending gang. Kits are available, but realistically they would be expensive ornaments. It is too easy to overcrowd.

With all my modelling, I bear in mind how people lived and worked at a particular time, and I try to create the spark the life. I consider why certain features are where they are, and why some things have survived.

Often, life can be suggested without hectic figures. The cycle by the church entrance suggests someone is inside, arranging flowers or polishing brass. Tools and equipment in certain places might mean the user has gone for a meal – or to the privvy!

The cattle wagons have bits of straw sticking out from the sides of empty wagons, other vehicles show evidence of previous loads. I think about footpaths and short cuts and why they exist where they do.

There is available a good range of figures, including some with moveable arms, legs and heads, whilst cutting and bending can alter others. However, I think position and grouping can make a picture some much more convincing.

Being conscious of time and age, I did not spent enough time on planning, and being too impulsive means changes have been inevitable. Due to so many changes of 17 or 18 years the wiring, some at least, is something of a rat's nest. Basically, the wiring is conventional and there is some interlocking of signals

A very clean and attractive visitor. An LMS 3-cylinder Compound Class 4P, a post grouping development of the original Johnson design for the Midland Railway on the turntable.

Class V2 No.4774 passes with a parcels train.

and points, and of course the crossing gates. David Hubbard and the late Colin Scoffin did a wonderful job in this department, with the utmost patience. There are faults now and again, and trying to reach them sometimes causes damage to signals, guy ropes, telegraph poles and chimneys – we are not as agile as we were. Hindsight is a wonderful thing!

The engine yard was a last project and everything was made accessible. If only this were so for the rest of the model, with motors underneath – it is not so much getting down as getting up again.

There are impossible wishes of course. I would love to hear the various sounds from different locomotives, the bells, telegraphs and levers in the signal boxes, the singing of the wires, and so on.

With time, thought, planning and money, I could have made fascias from the ceiling down to about two feet above the layout, with good back lighting and good access for cleaning. Perhaps I should have had just simple running lines, with lay by loops and engine yard – after all, trains moving through a landscape is my pleasure.

To sum up the project, the best words might be nostalgia, sentimentality, life experience and an interest in history.

The model is just a three dimensional picture, an impression with not too many features standing out from their surroundings, an attempt to recreate a scene from the past, of something long gone, and of the life which we shall never see again.

I think that creating an impression is so much easier if one has had sight and experience of the real thing. My model would not have proved as satisfying if I had had to rely on book knowledge alone.

My sincere thanks are due to the friends, alive and dead, who have supported and helped create this picture. Without their unstinting assistance it would never have happened.

Ex-GCR Class B3/1 No.6165 Valour *comes off the turntable. This loco was built by Robinson when he was CME of the GCR and re-built by the LNER after grouping.*

Elli Road Junction *Robin Griffiths*

Photos by Martin Dalling, description by Mike Marritt

Welsh industrial narrow gauge

This 6ft long by 18in wide 7mmNG layout is a perfect example of what is achieveable by a modeller new to the 7mm scale. Robin Griffiths is an experienced and prolific modeller in most of the smaller scales including 00 and 009, and more recently as a member of the N Gauge Society, in 2mm scale.

To jump from the latter to 7mm is quite a leap, but this 7mm narrow gauge layout proves that it is very possible with a bit of effort and imagination. The baseboard is constructed from fibre-board and all the scenery and buildings, plus the walling on the front of the layout is scratch-built. The latter is made from scribed Das. The trackwork is all Peco with electrical operation of the turnouts. The single loco used at present is built from a Sandbook kit, as is the other rolling stock. Sound is provided by Mylocosound chips, including the sounds of the working in the factory.

Robin is retired, so not subject to the exigencies of the working week, but he is a very prominent member of his local community being associated with local charities as well as being a local councillor. So the fact that he has produced a full working layout in the space of two months is quite a remarkable achievement, and should provide inspiration for other newcomers to the scale, particularly those who may be short of space and finance.

An end view of the complete layout.

Helen *busies herself around the yard.*

The trans-shipment shed and platform.

Helen *about to pick up wagons from the factory.*

The entrance to the factory.

Helen *moves a timber load to the unloading platform.*

Bucks Hill *by Kevin Wilson and friends*

Photos by Steve Flint courtesy of Railway Modeller

In the guise of Pontrilas

Model railways that take your breath away are seemingly few and far between these days. With ever finer modelling standards becoming the norm, new materials and techniques appearing in everyday use, and control systems that run layouts by themselves, conjuring up something truly masterful, unique and awe inspiring is ever more difficult.

Bucks Hill, however, must surely tick all those boxes. It's constructed to exacting 7mm fine standards, run via DCC to enable multiple train control and on-board sound and lighting effects, and features some of the most adroit scenic effects around.

It was therefore with eager anticipation that we ventured to Kevin Wilson's home to meet up with both Kevin and scenic and backscene specialist Paul Bambrick, for an exclusive insight into this exceptional railway layout. The story began unusually, not with the baseboards or the track and wiring, but with the backscenes…

Infinite depth

"I first became involved with the project whilst I was giving one of my backscene demonstrations at the Railex exhibition in Aylesbury. Bucks Hill had already been exhibited a few times in it's basic format and Kevin, and colleague Chris Gates, were trying to find the best way of adding a background and backscene to the existing scenic sections."

During that initial discussion, Kevin explained to Paul that he was looking for a means of attaching a backscene that flowed seamlessly from the 3D model. "It had to preserve perspective as convincingly as possible, and uphold an illusion of depth all the way to the horizon."

A few subsequent private meetings took place at which a basic backscene configuration was agreed. "We set about building a trial section to assess effectiveness, scale and colour." Paul said, explaining that the first area to be tackled was behind the elevated curve at the Abergavenny end of the layout; the section that would eventually have the longest panel. "Begun as a test bed, the design evolved into the construction prototype that all the remaining panels would eventually follow."

The backscene rear panels are made from 0.8mm sheet alloy, curved and riveted to a lightweight welded steel framework. These panels are positioned several inches away from the rear face of the baseboard on specially made steel frames which follow the contours of the corresponding baseboard.

The space between the board and the backscene panel helps to maintain a three dimensional effect and leaves room for fitting intermittent focal layers and forced perspective models, as Paul describes later

Holiday Haunts

The prodigious proportions and construction methods of Bucks Hill have rewritten many of the modelling maxims which we, as modellers, are so familiar with, so what driving force is there behind Kevin's vision?

"Well," he began, "I was leaning on the barrier watching the trains go by on Holiday Haunts, that popular O gauge layout based on Dawlish on the Devon coast. It had a full height backscene hiding the operators, and a constant flow of quality rolling stock. The crowds had long since dissipated, yielding some elbow room for the first time at that show. An equally appreciative friend Mike Morris interrupted my reverie and we enjoyed the view in silence for a while."

Those moments Kevin declared, sowed the seed that eventually became Bucks Hill. "I can't remember the exact year but it must have been in the early to mid 1990s."

The die was cast, his new project would be a 'roundy-roundy' and preferably portraying a real place. Mike volunteered to do some research and seek out a few possible locations. Kevin also wanted any length train to be accommodated in the fiddle yard without concern for exact location, to allowing for guest stock and the like.

He explained that Bucks Hill was planned as a prototypical location, featuring the requisite double tracked main line in a large oval for a complete through run in both directions, but would also include a branch line junction, adding the rider that; "…as with many deliberations of this nature a supply of ale from the local hostelry seemed to help, certainly with imagination, if not common sense…"

King Class 4-6-0 No.6011 King James I *on a north bound express.*

Eventually, Pontrilas in the Welsh Marches was deemed the best option, as it was GWR with LMS running rights, the junction for the Golden Valley line and had attractive buildings. "We changed the name to Bucks Hill in order to run anything and everything without critical observations, however, in retrospect we should have stuck with Pontrilas, as it is after all a pretty accurate representation, but there you are, too late now." The chosen period of history was to be the thirties, and the surrounding landscape would become the local rolling hills and valleys, with thriving rural communities in villages and farms.

In 7mm scale, the layout was planned as a pretty close representation of this outpost, the junction of the double tracked GWR/LMS joint main line between Hereford and Newport, and the single tracked Golden Valley branch line to Hay-on-Wye. Following the prototype, the main lines towards Abergavenny and Newport enter a short tunnel at the down end of the station, and emerge into the daylight again directly onto a short embankment broken with a stone occupation underbridge. The up scenic breaks are stone tunnels in cuttings as the two lines disappear in the Hereford, and Hay-on-Wye directions.

Making a start

Kevin designed and planned the project, working with Mike to construct the many plywood baseboards. The lower level station area ones are conventional, but each one was profiled to represent the undulating local landscape. Rising contours at either end were provided by plywood box sectioned boards, and the surface contours were all cut from inserted foam polystyrene blocks.

Steel trackwork was hand laid using C&L components fitted to stained wooden sleepers, gauged at 31mm between the platforms and through the straight stretches and pointwork at the station throat, encouraging stable running and closing the check rail gaps to finer standards. All the ground cover and detailing followed methodically over the next few years.

Most of the trackwork and some of the buildings were the work of the late Carl Legg. "Throughout the project and right up to his premature death, a stalwart supporter." Kevin remarked. "It was he who was adamant that we should target the Gauge O Guild 50th anniversary show in 2006 as our launch, which we achieved."

Metalwork and woodwork

Of the many disciplines involved in a project of this sort for me, loco building heads the satisfaction list, closely followed by the carpentry. "I realised early on that a full time job and a young family were not conducive to making all the rolling stock required so had to commission rolling stock. The coaches in particular," he said. "I hate doing them, you know; oh goody, only 40 door handles, 100 hinges and door stops to go…I would much rather do a loco!"

His workshop machinery has grown over the years with an assortment of lathes and milling machines. "I have only really been able to get on with this aspect since I retired, and I am eternally grateful to Tony Reynalds for all his help and instruction without which I would have struggled. Turning wheels and making crank axles is rewarding if a little nerve wracking now castings are no longer available."

Control and DCC

Kevin declared, "It is worth admitting at this juncture that I am an electronic dunce, and that without the help and encouragement of an expert in Adrian Newson, Bucks Hill would never have worked. He built the control panel and provided annotated wiring drawings and printouts for this said dunce to follow. As for DCC control, we had no previous experience of any of the systems. Indeed it was early days for DCC in the UK, but in the end we settled on Digitrax which was one of the manufacturers we felt would be around for the duration."

DCC was always a requirement from the outset but originally more as a management tool of the fiddle yard, "I didn't want to have to manage loads of sections. However it soon became apparent that the amount of walking involved inside a 50 foot layout was not helped by having manual route selection at either end of the fiddle yard. Consequently the yard was digitised with stationary decoders on the points and all routes could now be set from the hand held controllers." For a nominal cost Digitrax upgraded the tethered controllers to radio status enabling the operators to become static!

"The introduction of the high backscene posed a real problem." A 55-lever panel ran the scenic section from inside the layout, so, "…a 7 foot high back scene made viewing a tad difficult." Kevin admitted that it was with a very heavy heart that he took the wire cutters to over 36 50-way connecters, and installed another batch of stationery decoders. "How to replace the panel was solved by Chris Langdon, who organises the Missenden Abbey Railway Modellers weekend courses. One of the tutors, Pete Brownlow, was an expert on JMRI computer control software, he designed the mimic diagram and the route setting algorithms. Now with the help of a couple of video cameras in the fiddle yard I can run Bucks Hill entirely on my own."

Scenics and a forced perspective grid

"Thinking back," Kevin mused, "pretty much everything was a first on this project, so when it came to the scenery stage everyone looked at everyone else and shrugged their shoulders! It seemed sensible to ask a friend or two, so enter stage left Barry and Gill Norman, Gordon and Maggie Gravett, Chris Gates… and a case of red wine."

Pontrilas exemplified. The name was changed to Bucks Hill to allow the operators to run anything they like.

The scenery team grew and eventually when the question of the backscene arose, Paul Bambrick came aboard.

Paul explained that a diorama type presentation combining forced perspective with 3D textured surfaces is one of the best ways blending the undulating landscape contours of the layout into the background. "The initial mock up trial featured this method and Kevin agreed this would be the best and most realistic looking solution. A 3D backscene using a forced perspective grid is the best compromise for any model. It is the closest thing to a panoramic display, or a miniature artificial environment and as close as possible to the way that we naturally see the world around us."

"Forced perspective is only a modification of the familiar two dimensional perspective with vanishing points." Paul explained. "In simple terms, imagine drawing a feature onto a flat page in perspective, and then take a further step to fold the paper out and away from the page into three dimensions. By lifting the image out and away from the 2D page, an artificial, or forced 3D grid has been created, still using a horizon line like ordinary schoolbook two point perspective. The various vanishing points for the landscape features will all eventually be positioned along this horizon line. The rest of the scene concentrates on receding focal layers and relative sizes."

Paul described the 'receding focal layers' as one sided 'relief' panels positioned behind the railway boundary, they not made to scale, instead the elements diminish in relative size according to their perceived distance from the viewer.

Sounds and lighting

Kevin modified the original exhibition lighting rig to accommodate the high backscene and added a sound system to provide ambient noises. "There are as many as seven overlaid looped MP3 sound effects per section. The Abergavenny end concentrates on the sounds of the wildlife, birdsong, sheep and occasional bell practice from the village church in the distance; the forge and cottage has different birdsong; light rain showers match the squall of cloud on the backscene panel, and there's the occasional ring of the blacksmith's anvil."

Nearly all the locomotives have individual sound chips fitted and take their turn to drown out the ambient sounds as they pass.

GWR 17XX Class Pannier Tank No. 1873 with a featherweight load.

An overall view of the station area.

Epilogue

"In a general sense, yes," was Kevin's response to the question asking whether he considers Bucks Hill has achieved his original objectives.

"Would I change anything? Yes, the scenic boards should have been deeper front to back, and we could have made the backscene deeper in places as well."

He also acknowledged that in retrospect, choosing 31.5 mm track gauge might have been easier than the 31mm fine O gauge standards he adopted. He said that this was an aspect of the layout which needed quite a lot of fettling to get right.

The layout is now permanently located at home and, although theoretically portable, it is unlikely ever to be taken to exhibitions again. Asked if he would build another one to such grand proportions his answer was simple and unpropitious.

"I probably won't live long enough!"

The full transcript of this article first appeared in *Railway Modeller* January 2015 issue.

Figures are mostly from Chris Gates' character collection, painted using military modelling techniques. There are also some Aiden Campbell animals as well as figures from the Andy Duncan and Phoenix ranges.

There are a number of roads on the layout, usually surfaced with silver sand, and extended on to the backscene to blend in seamlessly.

King James I again, on a through express working to Hereford.

The buildings and structures were made by many contributors, and blend together very well. A variety of materials were used, including laminated styrene, and DAS scribed stone blocks.

The village church.

Ambient sounds of the church bells and the blacksmith enhance the experience for the onlooker.

The backscene trees are all constructed from twisted multi-strand copper battery cable, superglued for strength and dressed with Green Scene and Treemendus summer foliage materials.

Fen Drove *by John Hobden*

More Midland & Great Northern

Photographs by Paul Bason courtesy of British Railway Modelling

How can an average modeller produce a layout that others admire? Well, I'm the average modeller and rather flattered to be included in this publication. Fen Drove came about by looking at what some of the other contributors to this volume had achieved. They have shaped my philosophy and inspired me.

I think it is most important to believe in the concept, live the scene by getting under the skin of the people who created the real one or those who you imagined created the real one. If building something that did not exist in real life then make sure that it could have existed by creating a story to prove the possibility.

Make it believable by avoiding obvious clashes. Do your research thoroughly. Make everything to the same consistent standard.

Fen Drove is a small station which is part of a larger railway. When it is at home it is a through station which receives trains from one location and passes them on to another. It has its own freight traffic which has to be shunted when the pickup goods arrives. When at an exhibition the rest of the world is represented by a fiddle yard at each end and a much more intensive service is run.

The Fen Drove concept started with me looking at a space in the loft and trying to work out how to get a railway into it. Once that hurdle had been surmounted the next decision was what sort of railway. The rest of the system is rural and hilly so for contrast a section of flat fenland was chosen. The Fens are intensively farmed yet still bleak and remote and it was decided to try to capture the atmosphere of this unique landscape. Living in the Fens made research easy, or at least that was the theory, until I started searching for archetypal features such as the Railway Inn.

In the early stages of the project I had this crazy idea to create the whole

At one time Fen Drove had two feeder lines, one standard gauge still in use in the 1950s, and a narrow gauge. Specially for the photographer, one of the old wagons has been brought out of storage and Jabez Osler has brought his cart horse down to pose with it

The pedigree of the Midland and Great Northern joint is clear in this scene. Ivatt 4MT 43150, a typical M&GN workhorse of the 1950s is an LMS design, the signals and signalbox pure Midland and the coaches a development of original Gresley Great Northern designs.

The 4MTs were equally at home on freight and passenger working. This freight from Wisbech to Spalding would load potatoes during the autumn. In summer it would be carrying fruit and vegetables grown in the fertile Fen soil.

Surprisingly, railways were easier to build on the Fens than roads. This led to a number of feeder lines, some narrow gauge, being built to bring produce from the fields to the main lines. The Fen Drove Farmers Company line was a standard gauge example. Here Fen Drove Farmers No.2 Conundrum, a Hudwell Clarke locomotive of the same design as the preserved Wissington, shunts vans in the yard.

This scene suggests that the Great Eastern has completely taken over the M&GN. F5 locomotive is in charge of a train of former main line stock now relegated to secondary use and carrying the drab brown livery of their twilight years (D&S kits).

Locomotives of Great Eastern Railway origin could be seen on M&GN metals between 1936 and closure. This E4 is seen arriving from Spalding with a morning passenger service for Wisbech.

The trusty Ivatt 4MT eases her train out of Fen Drove towards Wisbech. Two coaches are more than sufficient for the passenger traffic

The E4 trundles in with the afternoon service from Wisbech probably bringing home pupils from the local secondary school.

scene in black and white. Let me tell you there are more than 50 shades of grey and some of then you would not want to try to reproduce. Besides, the trains would come in from the rest of the world in glorious technicolour and that would look like some of the strange effects you see in films – but is that such a bad idea? A model railway is actually an art form and the most successful ones make use of artistic and stage techniques to challenge the viewer's perception of the scene and draw them into thinking this is actually reality.

We are creating a caricature of a real or imagined scene so the truth can be distorted for effect but the truth must always be the inspiration for any effects we create. I spent many hours searching through books, online, and travelling round the countryside trying to establish what the key characteristics of a Fen landscape in winter were.

Once these basic characteristics had been established then the technical side of creating buildings from measurements and photos could begin. I like to start from measurements even if I later deviate for effect. I tried to ensure that all

The B12 is an unusual visitor to Fen Drove. On the main M&GN line they hauled the Yarmouth to Leicester expresses and were popular with their drivers though their firemen found the long fireboxes a challenge.

The Midland Railway supplied signalling equipment to much of the M&GN, particularly the western section. The Fen Drove box is still painted in the M&GN colour scheme of tan and stone.

The single line sections of the M&GN used Whittaker tablet catching apparatus to allow transfers at speed. One of these had to be included on the model and of course had to be fabricated from scratch.

The Railway Inn was a joy to build from styrene sheet and involved a lot of first hand research, especially into the interior! Figures by Omen and others with beer crates from wargaming diorama suppliers complete the scene.

The Fen Drove Dyke collected water from the surrounding fields which was then pumped into the oddly named 'Lady Nunn's Old Eau' (yes, that's a real name!) by the 'Fen Drove Engine'. These waterways are rich in fish, especially eels and the best way to move around them is by punt.

It's a lonely life on a remote Fen farm so when farmers bring their produce to the station yard for loading onto the trains it is a chance to catch up on local gossip. The ubiquitous 'Fergie 35' has largely replaced horses in the Fen by the 1950s

Everyone in the Fens owned a bike in the 1950s and small quantities of produce such as the string of onions seen here would be carried around on the handlebars, rather like the 'Johnny Onions' sellers who would come over from France.

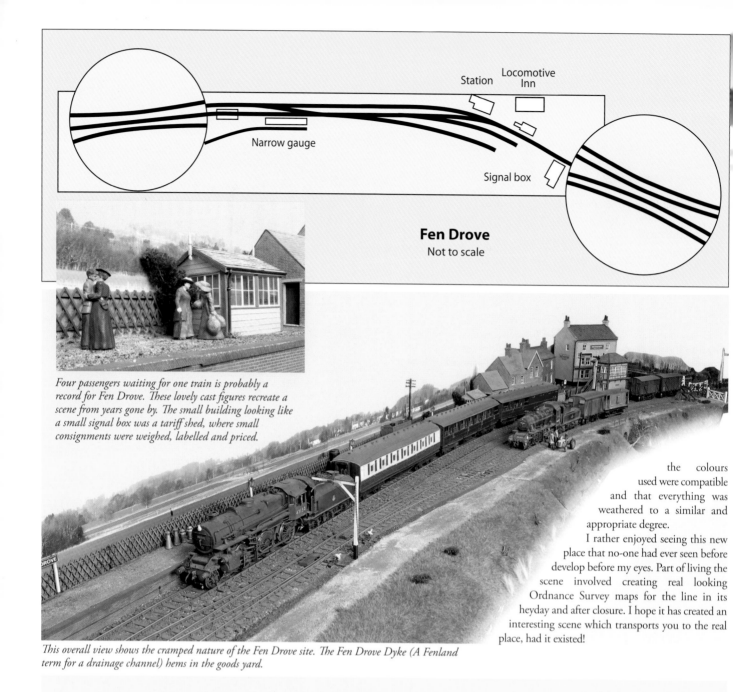

Fen Drove
Not to scale

Station
Locomotive Inn
Narrow gauge
Signal box

Four passengers waiting for one train is probably a record for Fen Drove. These lovely cast figures recreate a scene from years gone by. The small building looking like a small signal box was a tariff shed, where small consignments were weighed, labelled and priced.

the colours used were compatible and that everything was weathered to a similar and appropriate degree.

I rather enjoyed seeing this new place that no-one had ever seen before develop before my eyes. Part of living the scene involved creating real looking Ordnance Survey maps for the line in its heyday and after closure. I hope it has created an interesting scene which transports you to the real place, had it existed!

This overall view shows the cramped nature of the Fen Drove site. The Fen Drove Dyke (A Fenland term for a drainage channel) hems in the goods yard.

A very busy time at Fen Drove. The passenger hauled by 61540 passes a train of vans hauled by 46403, a Kettering engine on loan to South Lynn shed.

The Reely Grate Manufacturing Company

by Mike Bragg - Lots of layout in a very small space

Photographs by Chris Nevard courtesy of British Railway Modelling

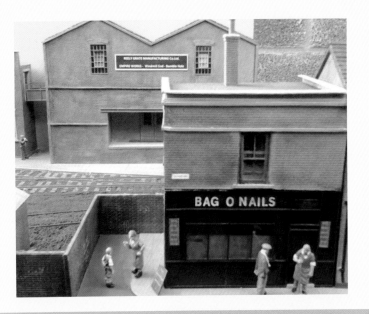

The Reely Grate Manufacturing Company is an O gauge micro-layout depicting a small yard serving the manufacturing company. It occupies a space of less than a square metre and demonstrates that you don't need acres of room to enjoy O gauge. The location of the factory and yard is Hammer Lane Windmill End near to the Bag o' Nails Pub in an area known as the Bumble Hole and yes, there really is a place called the Bumble Hole!

Construction

The baseboard is 1.5 x 0.5m constructed of good quality pine framing and a plywood top. The track work has been made from Peco (OO) code 100 flat bottom rail and copper-clad sleepers to give an industrial feel. The inlaid track has been constructed by soldering some of the rail on its side into the web of the running rail a sort of tram track arrangement. The traverser which is part of the main board runs on drawer runners, the middle track can line-up to each of the outer tracks which allows wagons to be run-round. The buildings are The Factory Complex, the Bag o' Nails pub and a row of terraced houses, all constructed from 2mm plywood skinned with plain or embossed plastic card. The pub although freelance apparently bears a striking resemblance to one of the same name in Bristol, and there's me thinking it was unique. The pub is

the only full depth building on the front of the layout. The terraced houses are fronts and roofs only as they conceal the traverser. These houses are based on those that stood in Birmingham Street, Stourbridge until demolished to make way for the ring road. The houses don't have door knobs as they had latches, hence the saying, latch-key kid. Creating this little community is just an attempt in making the scene believable. Why a pub? Well there was a tradition of foundry workers having a beer ration to replace the fluid lost whist working in a hot environment, so Joe would have had a steady income from Reely Grate. The head shunt is concealed by the display board which has the name and details of the layout including some larger versions of the signs outside the pub and on the goods inwards building.

Operation

Basically it involves just shunting a few wagons about using a waybill card system an operation which can take more than just a few minutes. Although simple it gives a lot of pleasure to operator and viewer alike. Uncoupling is achieved using strategically placed permanent magnets set in the ballast, all the stock have modified OO Hornby couplings, simple, effective and easy to operate.

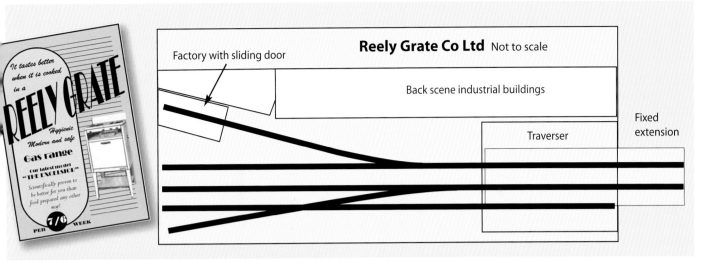

Reely Grate Co Ltd Not to scale

Factory with sliding door

Back scene industrial buildings

Traverser

Fixed extension

Ashwood Basin *by Mike Bragg*

Photographed by John Greathead

Black Country industry in a small space.

Ashwood Basin was on the Staffordshire & Worcestershire Canal and was the western terminus of the Earl of Dudley's Railway system, dating back to its opening in 1829. Today virtually all signs of the railway tracks have disappeared and it is now a marina for pleasure craft. From Ashwood basin the line ran to Shut End, and the collieries at Corbyns Hall near Lenches Bridge. The railways main purpose was to convey coal to the canal and this continued until the NCB stopped sending Baggeridge coal to Stourport power station via the canal in October 1953. Set over two boards with the scenic section covering all of one and about a third of the other, the rest of the second board being a traverser running on ball bearing slides. The layout is an attempt to capture the essence of the area as opposed to a slavish copy of the prototype. Buildings have been constructed using different techniques. The garage is a simple plastikard shell finished with Slaters brick and signs printed on the computer. The villas are made from homemade plaster castings and hand carved before painting. The pub is from good quality artists' card with pre-stained scale size bass wood (lime) wooden beams applied and then fine casting plaster infill. The rustic factory is an anglicised Thomas Yorke kit heavily modified to suit the location. Because of the very simple nature of the layout several cameos have been included, some only the operators can see.

The loading point of the canal basin where the full wagons from the colliery were off-loaded into the narrow boats.

1901 Class 0-6-0 PT No. 1927 at the station platform.

The pub yard, with the barrels about to the sent to the cellar.

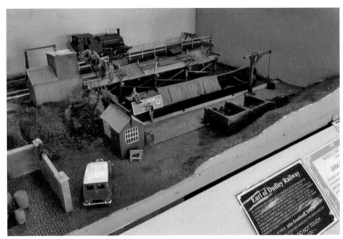

This superbly demonstrates the compact nature of the layout.

The 'end of the line.'

The station, there wasn't one in real life, is a simple platform and shelter (Bumble Hole Line) with access via steps and end ramp. The platform is surfaced using C&L ash ballast which was applied to dark grey paint rather than glue, although I have used a cheap un-scented hair spray as an extra hold.

The trestle is constructed from Evergreen plastic strip and scribed siding, the check rails being code 100 set against the chairs of the running rails.

There are two narrow boats in the basin, a loaded Joey and a Day Boat. The day boat *Jellicoe Number 2* is finished as a British Waterways boat as the canals had by this time been nationalised. Both these narrow boats have been constructed from plastikard. The day boat has a canvas sheet arrangement made from strips of single ply tissue paper stiffened with white glue and then painted with acrylics. In the background are the coal chutes based on those at Anglesey Basin near Cannock.

The water tank, a somewhat 'guess what the tank at Himley looked like,' (since found to be almost correct) is yet another simple plastikard structure, a sort of make it up as you go along, but it looks OK sort of thing.

Ground cover is a mixture of Woodland Scenics, Silfor tufts and Noch Wild electrostatic grass, the noch grass being applied via a homemade electrostatic applicator made from a tea strainer and a converted fly swat. I take no credit for the device as I found the prototype on the internet.

The 'Olde World' pub with its half-timbered architecture.

A passenger working arrives at the station platform.

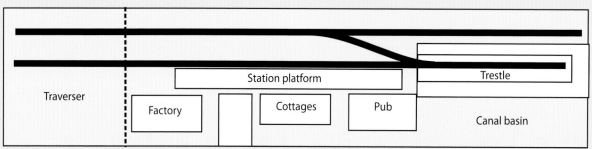

Ashwood Basin Not to scale

Traverser

Factory

Station platform

Cottages

Pub

Trestle

Canal basin

The pannier tank about the enter 'the trestle.'

North Witton *by Mike Sandell*

Photos by the owner

BR (NE) in North Yorkshire

North Witton is a small village at the head of a Pennine valley somewhere between Wensleydale and the Scottish borders. Despite its small size it retained a frequent service of passenger and freight trains into the early 1950s, with the latter serving the goods yard and the private sidings of the local quarry and timber yard.

The station on the first three baseboards dates back over 20 years when the layout was straight and the fiddle yard was a 6ft (1.8m) diameter turntable. A 4ft extension was added to avoid shunting directly onto the turntable, but this was too long to erect in the loft. So eventually an even grander extension saw the layout turned into a U-shape with non-scenic test track style narrow boards, and new storage sidings using points. The station baseboards are substantial and heavy structures, with a grillage of 2 x1in timber and chipboard running surface. The newer boards are much lighter using 6mm ply!

The locomotives in use are mostly of ex-NER origin, with the kits bought in most cases from their original producer, but now in other hands. The coaches shown are mostly Ian Kirk kits, but the corridor rake includes a Sparmac and a Sidelines kit. Wagons are all built from kits from the usual suspects. The station track is C&L (K&L) flexible track with the points built from their kits, powered by lemoco/fulgerex point motors. Fiddle yard track is a Peco/C&L mixture, and the Peco points are hand operated. As befits its age the layout is ordinary DC, with five sections all switchable between two hand held controllers.

Loading up at the timber yard.

Except for the engine shed, which is a plastic kit I managed to build myself, buildings have been scratch-built by fellow members of Birtley Model Railway Club. (I'm afraid buildings come well down the list of my modelling priorities). The station building is based on a small drawing of Fourstones on the Newcastle-Carlisle line in one of K Hoole's books, and the goods shed and signal box are copied from Bowes on the Stainmore line.

Ex-NER Class G5 LNER No. 67298 stands outside the engine shed awaiting its next duty.

Mineral wagons about to unload over the coal drops.

Ex-NER Class J27 heavy freight loco stands by the signal box.

Goods wagons mark time before being unloaded.

Empty bolster wagons arrive to pick up their load.

There's always time for a chat in a rural backwater like North Witton.

The G5 heads away from the station with a passenger working.

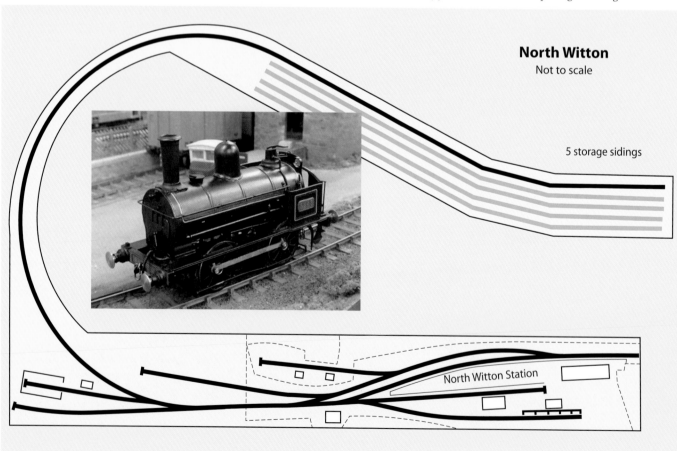

North Witton
Not to scale

5 storage sidings

North Witton Station

Helmthwaite & Chapel Lane - twice the fun

John Kneeshaw for St Neots MRC

Photos by Paul Bason by courtesy of British Railway Modelling

We think that too many model railways appear two dimensional with tracks running on a very flat earth; we wanted to make proper use of the third dimension, height; and build something a little different than the ordinary run of model railways. It had to be light enough to be taken to exhibitions without risking life and limb every time we picked up a layout section.

One of the major limitations of most end to end layouts is the presence of an obvious fiddle yard at one, or even both ends; a waste of valuable space for an Exhibition Manager, and a bit of blank board for the paying public. It was in trying to solve this problem of the obvious fiddle yard that we came up with the idea of building what was effectively two layouts in the same space, with the fiddle yard of each layout concealed behind or under part of the other layout. Hence a low level layout (Helmthwaite) and a high level layout (Chapel lane). In the 7.5 metres that we had allowed ourselves there was not enough space for a rail connection between the upper and lower layouts; the gradient would have been so steep as to require a rack.

There is a legend for our railway, but there isn't space for storytelling here. It called for a scene in urban West Yorkshire. The railways portrayed came into existence because of the industries already present in the town which was in a hilly area. Lack of space forced the LMS line into a very limited small valley only accessible by tunnelling beneath existing buildings. Later the GNR (now LNER) saw an opening and arrived in the same town from the East taking advantage of a high level route, and built the Chapel Lane Coal yard adjacent to but about twenty-five feet higher than the LMS line.

The vision

We wanted the model to work as a whole scene, even though it was to be a little over 7.5m (0.2 miles in O gauge) long, and so a lot of thought went into the views that would be available to an exhibition visitor. The track is about 1.3m above ground level in the Chapel Lane coal yard and 165mm lower at Helmthwaite. It naturally followed that the buildings at the Helmthwaite Station end of the layout would have to be tall enough to both hide the fiddle

Helmthwaite Goods Yard is sited about 25 scale feet below Chapel Lane Coal Yard. The two are linked by the hydraulic powered inclined plane wagon lift.

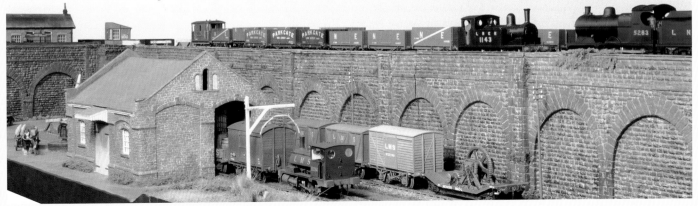

Helmthwaite Goods shed with Chapel Lane coal yard above.

LMS 3F No 7660 emerges from beneath the bridge on the approach to Helmthwaite Station while above it J11/3 No 5283 positions a brake van in the LNER coal yard.

sidings of Chapel Lane, and allow us room to manipulate stock below them. The roof of the taller of the two dominant buildings is 1.7m above floor level, and therefore rarely features on photographs of the layout. The end of the layout containing the modelled area of Chapel Lane Coal Yard, with Helmthwaite Goods Yard below it, might have lacked interest had we not come up with the unique selling point of the layout, an inclined wagon hoist.

The height of the layout may be a little inconvenient for small children, but we dislike models that seem to provide nothing but views of coach roofs.

We also wanted to get away from the straight line of boards that typify so many exhibition layouts, so we devised a plan in which the layout is bent in the middle so that an observer standing front centre has the scene wrapping around him. This bend in the plan has certainly worked in terms of views of the layout, but it made track planning trickier, especially in terms of the radius of curvature of the entry road to the lower fiddle yard, which sits under Chapel Lane Coal Yard.

Modelling the model

Before we built anything we made several sketches of what we wanted the railway to look like, and then I made a 1:20 scale model of the model so that we could get a better and more three-dimensional idea of what we were trying to do. This is something I'd never done before; it wasn't anything exotic, just some thin plywood and stiff cardboard glued together to make a 3D shape onto which the proposed tack plan was drawn. It served its purpose because the plans, the model and our proposed budget were approved by the club and we were allowed to start the project.

Foundations

Having taken account of our storage space limitations, we designed our baseboards using composite beams constructed from two lengths of 50mm wide x 5mm thick plywood spaced apart by 20mm softwood blocks. These are remarkably strong do not flex at all. The plan that was evolved needed three sections measuring 1250 x 900mm, two sections half that size (625 x 900mm), and two trapezoidal sections that were effectively 1250 x 900mm with the ends sliced off an angle of around twelve degrees. The beams were screwed and glued together to make open bases rather like the timber framing of a traditional baseboard.

Next a second layer of structure was created with an upper surface 170mm above the lower sections for the upper layout. We had now built seven open baseboards with no surface on which to lay our track or build our world. Plywood bases just wide enough for the track were screwed and glued to the beams only where we needed to lay track, the scenic areas were built onto very flimsy ply or card, and some of the buildings have no substructure at all; this was all part of the weight saving strategy to save our middle-aged (and older) backs. For storage and transportation, four of the base sections pack face to face in pairs and the two half bases (that form each end section of the layout) bolt

end to end facing the one remaining large section. Thus the layout sections pack away into three sections of 1250 x 900 x 520mm. The legs are simple planed softwood double crossed H sections with screw adjusters on each foot. The tops of the legs slot into softwood sockets built into the layout sections. The legs are further stabilised by diagonal braces. When assembled the layout sections are aligned by cabinet maker's dowels that were installed before and track bases were laid. Despite not actually being baseboards in the traditional sense, we still continue to refer to them as boards.

Track plan

The final track plans for the lower (Helmthwaite) layout was arrived at with the aid of pencils, turnout templates, some O gauge locos and stock and several rolls of wallpaper. We knew what we wanted the final track plan to look like, but the tricky bits were getting the pointwork clear of the joints between sections of the layout, keeping the radius of curves big enough to avoid buffer locking problems, and keeping the platform road, loco run round/ head shunt and sidings in reasonable proportion to each other so that we didn't make operation impossible. Also, because we were only going to lay substantial base where there was track, we had to be absolutely confident that we had a track plan that worked. It was fortunate that we had agreed that all of the track would be hand built and that we wouldn't therefore be constrained by the geometry of commercially produced pointwork.

By the time that we moved on to the final plan for the upper (Chapel Lane) part of the system I had acquired a copy of Templot (www.templot.com), a wonderful track planning programme, produced by 85A Models (Martin Wynne). It is the most complete and most flexible bit of model railway software

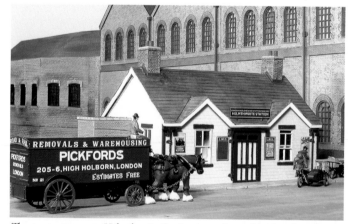

The street entrance to Helmthwaite Station is on the road bridge above the railway. 1930s local road traffic was still dominated by horse power. The equine-propelled vehicle was built from a kit by Duncan Models. The whole scene is dominated by the three storey Osborne engineering works.

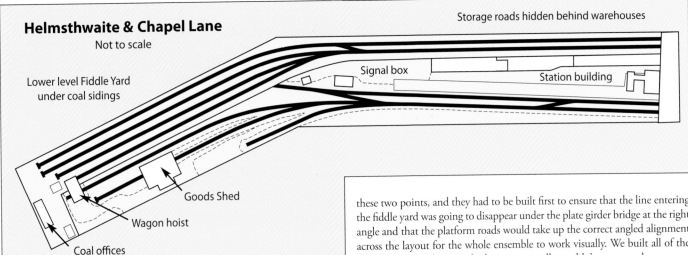

Helmsthwaite & Chapel Lane

Not to scale

Lower level Fiddle Yard
under coal sidings

Storage roads hidden behind warehouses

Signal box

Station building

Goods Shed

Wagon hoist

Coal offices

I have yet come across. It needs some time and effort to learn how to use it because it is a little non-intuitive, but it made the final track plan for Chapel Lane easier than the one for Helmthwaite, and I was able to print a full scale template for the whole of the upper level.

Trackwork and S&T

Since we had set ourselves the task of hand building the entire track, C&L Finescale was, at the time, the obvious place to look. Because we are not a wealthy club, we eschewed the readymade Vs, crossings and switches, and bought a lot of yards of nickel-silver rail, bags and bags of running chairs, and enough slide chairs for the point work. The adoption of hand built track work allowed us to build custom pointwork that would fit the flow of the layout. This was especially valuable when working in a limited space since curved points could be built to any radius we chose (all 5ft 6in or larger, except the brake van siding to save space).

The lower layout trackwork was built first starting with the most difficult pieces on the whole model, the three-way point and the slightly curved point that joins it to, and splits the line arriving from the fiddle yard. These points sit at the centre of the plan. Although it seemed rather strange to some of the group to start with the most difficult bits, all the other track work flowed from

these two points, and they had to be built first to ensure that the line entering the fiddle yard was going to disappear under the plate girder bridge at the right angle and that the platform roads would take up the correct angled alignment across the layout for the whole ensemble to work visually. We built all of the pointwork directly onto the layout; we really couldn't see any advantage to building points off the layout and then trying to align them later.

The points are operated by rods and model aircraft bell-cranks situated under the track bases. The final connection to the point blades is by turnout operating units slightly modified from a method described in *Model Railway Journal* (2002, No 139, p297). The two points forming the platform crossover are operated by a single Tortoise machine mounted on its side driving two of the turnout operating units via more rod and bell-crank linkages. It is therefore impossible for the operator to reverse one point while the other remains in the normal position.

The trackwork on the upper (Chapel Lane) layout was a breeze in comparison with our earlier work, because I use printed templates generated in Templot. Those templates are still there, hidden under track, ballast, coal and ash. The point operation mechanisms for Chapel Lane are a lot less complex than those for Helmthwaite. The layout is so high and the view of most of the track is obscured by the parapet wall of the stone arches so we went for surface rodding operated by sprung ground levers manufactured by Caboose Industries in the US. The HO scale version is much smaller that the O scale model and gives more than enough throw for a finescale O gauge point.

There are two operating L&Y pattern lower quadrant signals built from MSE kits built by Chris Dales. The signals are operated from the main lever frame and use our usual arrangement of rodding and bell-cranks.

A three coach local train pulls into Helmthwaite in the shadow of Helmthwaite Mills and the adjoining Osborne Engineering.

Control

A little while after we started building Helmthwaite and Chapel lane I changed my home layout from analogue control to digital, using a Lenz DCC system. Despite that change, the fledgling exhibition layout was wired for a cab control analogue system with enough switched sections to allow for almost any operational requirement. Connections between boards were made with multi-way Q type pin and socket connectors. The layout was fully tested in this format and two control panels were built, one clipping onto the front of the layout and the other (for the upper layout) integral with the back of the layout. The upper and lower layouts were treated as two independent railways. As time passed another member of our little band moved to DCC control, and we changed the layout to DCC. It wasn't a hard choice, those of us with experience of DCC realised how flexible it was and how much easier it is to run, or leave stationary, any engine anywhere you wanted; and we were able to use subtly muted sound decoders in certain locos to add a bit more atmosphere. The conversion was easy; we simply fed the track output of the DCC into the control panel and turned all the section switches on and left them that way. We could run both layouts very happily with one DCC setup, but because we had two available we chose to run two completely independent systems, one on Chapel Lane and the other on Helmthwaite; that way a short on one layout won't stop the other layout from running. There is a hand throttle available for each operator and with the help of a connection to a laptop we can have wireless running with smartphones acting as throttles.

The wagon hoist

This was entirely my fault. I was reading Bob Essery's book, *The London Tilbury and Southend Railway and its Locomotives*, and I came across, on page 41, a photograph of the inclined wagon hoist at Leystonstone. The Leytonstone hoist was built by the Hydraulic Company of Chester and installed in 1905. Its function was to move wagons between two levels, separated vertically by 20-25ft, on a site where there was no room for a banked track. Despite it being a long way from East London to West Yorkshire, it seemed that a copy of the inclined hoist would serve several purposes. It would give us a way of moving full coal wagons arriving in the LNER's Chapel Lane yard down to the LMS system below, it would give us a point of real interest at the end of the layout furthest from the station. Interestingly I later discovered, but never confirmed, reports of a similar inclined wagon hoist being built in the Leeds area.

A full description of my design and build of the 7mm scale version would make a book chapter article in itself, so I will summarise it as being scratch-built out of brass and nickel-silver, propelled by an Archimedean drive, and featuring automatic stop at the top and bottom. I enjoyed embellishing it with the correct pattern railings and copying the original notice – 'NOTICE Load not to exceed 23 Tons. This hoist is not to be used for passengers'. The control cabin at the top of the hoist, and the man operating it were modelled by Keith Gowen. The photos of the hoist show it to be a fair copy of the original.

The wagon hoist has been so popular at exhibitions that we have had to provide a dedicated hoist operator to keep the public happy.

The first floor station interior modelled by Jacqui Younger has now been further enhanced by internal lighting.

Scenics and buildings

The first scenic adventure was painting the track which was painstakingly done with Humbrol Track Dirt and Phoenix Light Rust enamels. We then moved on to the ballasting of the lower layout; this was not quite the success we had planned. Technically it was unadventurous; nice small dark stone chipping were painstakingly placed with fingers and paint brushes and then stuck down with dilute PVA glue, being very careful not to gum up the turnout operating units. This process took three or four of our weekly sessions and then we stood back and admired it. After a couple of weeks when further work was progressing elsewhere on the railway I said to a couple of the guys, "I don't really like the colour of that ballast. It's too dark". Everybody else then said that they thought the same, but had been reluctant to speak up because they thought everyone else was happy with it. So every bit of the dark ballast was wetted and extracted with old chisels, craft blades and blasphemy. The re-ballasting was carried out with much lighter coloured granite chips sold as OO gauge, but measuring around 1 – 1.5in in 7mm scale. It was real pain, but none of us would have ever been happy with the original ballast.

The vision called for some very large buildings. These and the station buildings were all scratchbuilt by the group. The obvious scenic feature; the retaining wall of 14 stone arches that separates the upper and lower layouts was made using very light vacuum formed plastic parts from Langley Models.

Wagons in Helmthwaite yard being unloaded by the hand crane.

We did think about casting our own, but the weight would have been a real problem to us. Painting these stone arches was a bit of an education. In order to get the finish I wanted, painting turned out to be a five stage process from priming to the final dry brushing of highlights, with drying time in between each process.

The job of supervising ground scenics, road surfaces and grassed areas went to Keith Gowan, who set the standard for our scenic work. Most of the vehicles were built by me, but the beautiful carthorses were all painted by Jacqui. The Helmthwaite section of the layout has been greatly enhanced by the addition of cosmetic point rodding, and signal wires and pulleys; a task readily undertaken by a more recent recruit to our group.

Locos and stock

Traffic on the layout has been kitbuilt and many of the engines are now sound equipped.

In conclusion

Helmthwaite & Chapel Lane has been seen at the NEC and at Guildex as well as many shows in the East. It is still active on the exhibition circuit.

An elegant covered stairway gives passenger access to the platform at Helmthwaite. The recently (1937) installed baggage is lift out of view on the right of the building.

Leeton

Greater Manchester in the 1950s

by John Ditchfield

Stanier Class 3 MT 2-6-2T leaves Leeton with a local passenger train.

Leeton came about following a decision to change to 7mm scale from an extensive OO gauge system installed in an attic room, which provided a lot of engaging operation, if not technically or scenically to the latest standards. In fact, as construction started in 1988, the new layout does not incorporate all the latest tech either. Whereas the OO gauge was fixed in the room the new layout was to be portable with a view to going to exhibitions.

An initial scale plan showed that, while the room was a great size for OO at 16 x 8ft (not got as far as metric yet!), achieving an interesting layout in 7mm was going to be challenging. A quick survey showed that the existing room could be widened to give 12ft at the widest part although still restricted to 8ft at the narrow end due to brickwork – hence the horseshoe shape of the layout.

The track diagram was drawn out, via several different versions, full scale on thick cardboard, ensuring radii, clearances, train lengths etc. These card templates then test fitted into the available space. Baseboards are made of plywood aligned with pattern-maker's dowels and held together with coach bolts. A strong method of construction which has needed no repair over the many times the layout has been assembled and dis-assembled. Each board was made to an individual shape to fit the cardboard plan. All the pointwork was also pre-built onto the cardboard plan so almost everything fitted together first time and fitted onto the baseboards.

Now how to make sure the new layout would be fun to operate – in my opinion only of course.

The layout requires operators to shunt and make up trains to be sent to each other. This also applies in the fiddle yard where all movements are along trackwork and none by picking up models. On a small end to end layout 3-link couplings would drive me mad. Stock on Leeton is fitted with Sprat & Winkle couplings after trials of the different types available. They have been modified with heavier links and are actuated by electromagnets within station limits and also with some fixed magnets in the fiddle yard. The use of the delay facility of the couplings means the whole layout runs hands off except for assigning wagon loads.

Double track operation was considered highly desirable along, with goods yard movements separate to the station area. The layout keeps three people busy through a sequence timetable which represents a full working day and which takes a minimum of two hours to complete. Both the station and fiddle yard areas are divided into control zones and are operated under the principle that movements are controlled by the destination operator. It's therefore quite easy to arrange traffic arriving and departing the station area at the same time.

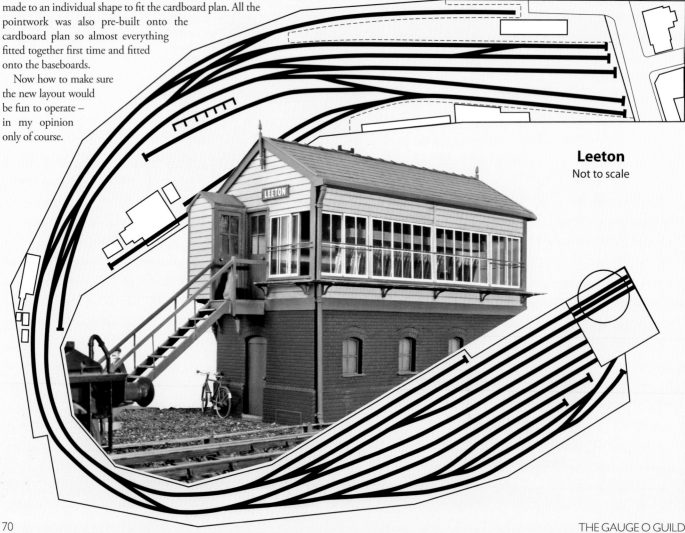

Leeton
Not to scale

A Class 4F shunts the coal yard whilst Jinty 0-6-0T No. 47312 leaves Leeton with a single coach local train.

Due to the small space available, in O gauge terms that is, we also need to inject some imagination to support the high traffic flow. Leeton is imagined to be the terminus of a line from Bolton and Manchester portrayed as in 1959. Just beyond the tunnel is a branch to a smaller town of Gibfield served by motor train and daily goods train from Leeton. The motor train mostly connects with Bolton & Manchester passenger services at Leeton. Also to be imagined is a small loco shed.

Central to the goods operation is that all loads are removable (no coal wagons going into the coal road full and then going back again just as full). Wagon movements are controlled by coloured pins attached to the wagons. The pins are allocated by the Station and Fiddle Yard operators giving variety for the Goods Yard operator. As example the early morning goods arrives at Leeton with wagons displaying red pins for unloading in the Yard and others having blue pins which need to be marshalled into the branch goods for Gibfield. Occasionally a wagon arrives with a black pin which needs to be trip worked to the loco shed.

Overall view of the Leeton station area with the Stanier tank about to retire to the shed.

Primrose Hill *by Mike Bragg*

Photos by Chris Neveard courtesy of British Railway Modelling

Small layout with style

Once located in Netherton, was a firm of chain makers, Noah Hingley & Sons, which was famous for making the anchors for the ill-fated Titanic. The works were set up by Noah Hingley in 1837 on the banks of the Dudley No. 2 canal. Anchor manufacture commenced in 1848 and the works were extended in 1852. The main anchor for the Titanic weighed fifteen and a half tons and, on completion, was hauled from the factory to the rail head at Dudley Port by 20 shire horses

owned by a local ostler called Edward Newman. Hingleys also produced anchors for the Lusitania and a number of other ocean liners. A replica of the anchor now stands on the old marketplace. Hingleys' success in international

Mike Bragg, a well respected builder of micro-layouts, with Primrose Hill as it appears when at exhibitions.

markets and their use of the Netherton name for their trademarked wrought iron products (e.g. Netherton Crown Special Best Iron) caused the name of Netherton to be known more widely both in the UK and overseas. A sculpture of an anchor stands at the junction of Castleton Street and Halesowen Road. This commemorates the local anchor and chain industry and the anchor motif can be found in a number of places around Netherton including the metal park benches in Netherton Park, immediately adjacent to the works of Noah Hingley & Sons on the Dudley.

The model

Primrose Hill occupies a space about that of an ironing board, 55 x 18in, stands 36in high and has integral fold-up legs. The main focus of the layout is the buildings, caricatures of Lloyds Proving House, Noah Hingleys including the transhipment shed and a Black Country pub The Round of Beef. Perhaps the most notable building is a version of the Crossing Keepers/Signal Cabin that was situated on the Holy Bank and Hilton Main Colliery Railway. Although nowhere near the Saltwells Branch it is such a unique building I just had to

Time for a gossip amongst the locals.

incorporate it the overall scheme. I've bent, massaged and altered so much that I ought to try and get something almost right. However, on the down side, in this case not a railway term, I have discovered that the photo showing a transhipment shed in Primrose Basin is not in fact part of the Earl's railway. The Earl's Basin, Primrose 2, had no railway connection, oh well as they say rule 1 applies - it's my railway.

The buildings are constructed from 2mm Lite-ply which is very easy to shape and cut and then skinned with embossed plastic-card. The baseboard is built from good quality 75 x 25mm pine framework with a 6mm ply top all glued and screwed. The traverser which allows locomotives to run round their train slides on ball bearing runners. The track is code 100 flat bottom rail soldered on copper-clad sleepers and the single point is 34in radius; ferrite permanent magnets are set at suitable locations to operate the auto couplings.

A selection of scratch-built buildings on the layout.

Allendenac *by Richard Chown*

Photographed by the author unless indicated

Fulfilling a dream in O gauge

I always wanted accurate models of bridges, building a Brunel fan viaduct while still at school, after which I thought of the elegant French viaducts. At the end of my career in 1991 I set out to fulfil that dream: to build a portable layout with a viaduct, using Scaleseven/Proto 43,5 standards – the only sensible way when tackling a new project. The prototype chosen is Rouzat Viaduct, over the Sioule, one of four on the Paris-Orléans company's line from Montlucon to Gannat. Every possible rivet, more than half a million, is modelled. This would be something spectacular, with the wow factor that I believe such layouts should have.

Is it: a) a display of interesting techniques, b) all too much, c) an abject failure: or all three at the same time? You decide. Optimistically I incline to the first, and was encouraged when Loco-Revue in *Réseauxrama 2* called it 'un coup de théâtre.' They also called the team 'les saltimbanques,' a travelling circus.

There were design problems. Any decent model railway is built in three dimensions. Could one be put together from components that are mostly two-dimensional, with at least one of those dimensions reduced to the minimum? Then they might pack tight, just the fragile fully modelled parts segregated.

Those key artistic elements, the spaces between, can shrink to occupy a space little larger than the singularity from which all matter came. The track and the scenery can be transported and supported separately, the scenic surfaces can be fabric rolled out. Buildings remain three dimensional but can be designed to pack inside one another like Russian matrioska dolls. Would it peg together? No more hunting for those bolts and wingnuts – always lying at the other end of the layout. Just a few screws needed for final adjustments.

Supporting the general level are the fold-flat legs that Harold Crabtree devised for the first West Lancs O Gauge Group layout in the late 1950s, here made 1m wide. Bracing their tops creates a space frame whose bottom link is the friction of the floor. The crossbeams added increase the stiffness and carry the trackbeds (there are no baseboards as such), the buildings and the supports for the scenery. A scenic surface of latex impregnated nylon voile is supported by upholstery foam glued with carpet adhesive to 10mm MDF sheet lying on the crossbeams, stiffened where found to sag under its own weight. More latex secured the woodland scenics.

The viaduct required a different approach. Its deck is continuous over three spans; that is how the prototype is done, there is no escape. The box that the deck travels in is thus also the base upon which the whole thing is assembled.

PO No. 646 le Mammouth *on the wye, Scaleseven on 42in radius.*

The prototype, Rouzat Viaduct, looking west.

The green shed.

Rouzat Viaduct in 7mm scale. Photo: Gerard Tombroek, Rail Miniature Magazine, *Antwerp*

Yet another train crosses the viaduct, headed by Genghis Khan.

Photo: Allan Goodwillie

The town rises behind the station, in the foreground PO 0-6-0 NO. 857 Genghis Khan *sets back round the wye.*

Photo: Gerard Tombroek, Rail Miniature Magazine,

It is 16ft long, and the main constraint on transport. The deck alone needs two people to lift it during assembly; it must be one of the heaviest etched kits ever. There are rail breather (expansion) switches at both ends of the viaduct deck, there as much to cope with the fitting of the deck as with expansion.

Track level, 5ft above the floor, is defined by the viaduct height. Eye level is also horizon level. Behind the station rising scenery hides the horizon. Towards and behind the viaduct however there are overlapping painted hardboard backscenes representing the hills upstream, selectively compressed. The valley rises above the tunnel exit leading to the fiddle yard. Behind all this is a continuous canvas backcloth hung from 10mm steel rods at 20in centres, its top being 11ft 6in above the floor. This layout carries as much canvas as a medium size yacht, at risk from wind when loading bay doors are open

The layout is lit as one scene with stage lighting spots on stands set up across the aisle. It is intended to be seen in a variety of ways, the whole thing as a single scene, local views, close ups with more detail, even to individual blades

Road vehicles: The ox cart, from an Atelier Belle Époque kit, oxen converted brutally from Andy Duncan's cows.

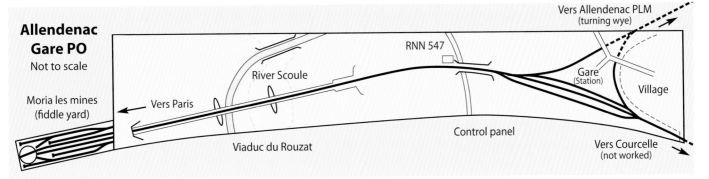

Allendenac Gare PO

Not to scale

Moria les mines (fiddle yard)

Vers Paris

River Scoule

Viaduc du Rouzat

RNN 547

Control panel

Vers Allendenac PLM (turning wye)

Gare (Station)

Village

Vers Courcelle (not worked)

In the station.

of grass in places. There is a place where you can see the locos right before your eyes, another where you can only see the top of the train as it moves. You can touch; there are rostrums in places to help shorter people (and the operators), and there is a periscope for wheelchair users. There is a short rope barrier at the viaduct only, to keep people at the best viewing distance, and to prevent anyone from tripping and falling against it. Interestingly ladies, and children, seem to understand the layout better than men, and the purpose of the periscope always has to be explained.

The name Allendenac (the spring of Allenden) is un hommage to Dennis Allenden, inspirational modeller and writer of the 1960s and 70s, lost to us at an early age. The period is c1880. Operation is simple as there is just one demand from the viewers 'when is the next train going over the viaduct?' The worked autocouplings are Richard Tarpie's Lincs, using permanent magnets. The unworked couplings in the carriage sets were a bother until changed to three link – this is an exhibition layout first and foremost.

I succeeded in building the layout while I was still capable and it ran satisfactorily at six of the eight exhibitions it attended, including Orléans in 2010. Now I no longer have the stamina. Who would like to buy a viaduct?

Yet another train crosses the viaduct, headed by P-O 0-6-0T No.1001 l'Hippopotame,

Photo: Jim Summers

Starting to put it together at Houten, putting up legs and cross beams.

Ready to lift the viaduct at Perth.   Photo: Jim Summers

Lifting into place.   Photo: Jim Summers

Bruce Murray attends to a problem through a rabbit hole.   Photo: Jim Summers

The layout erected at Houten NL 2010. Ian Everett and Mike Walshaw prepare for duty.

Oakwood Furnaces
by *Richard Chown*

Photographs by the author.

Scaleseven in a small space

This layout was built primarily as a diorama, to the set maximum of 900 in sq for the competition at Guildex 2006. On considering the Rules I realised straight away that it would be possible to create an operational layout in such a space and this is the result. It is 4ft 6in long, curving back and front and self-contained, there is no detachable fiddle yard.

I have created part of a wagon repair works among the remains of an iron works, a 'might have been' in South Wales circa 1900. What you see here is the 'finished' end of the workshop with repaired and freshly painted wagons emerging, pushed out of the doors by hand. The locomotive takes them and then pushes them out of sight to the main line end, through the remains of the old rolling mill at the back. Still standing are the old furnaces and the blowing engine house. It is a scene of rust and decay, for emphasis the loco is deliberately painted a bright colour. The wagons under repair are mostly black for Glyncorrwg Colliery, the main customer, a few others in different colours add their excitement to the scene.

Alex Jackson auto-couplings are used, here are only required to couple. The wagons cope with the 9in radius curves because they are all the same length. The wagons are all Slater's/Powsides kits, with suspension modified, using plastikard, to equalise one axle per wagon. No weathering was needed as they appear fresh out of the shop. The locomotive, known as *Pugsy*, however is scratch-built, the prototype coming from a side view published in *The Chronicles of Boulton's Siding* by Alfred Rosling Bennett, published in 1927.

The layout is operated from the right hand side and has been to several exhibitions.

Shunting an unpainted wagon from one road to another.

Pulling out of the front road.

Pugsy and a visiting wagon above the culvert.

The old gaffer has come down with his dog. Come a long way and brought his chair and the hut with him. He is a french figure kit, and the hut is a Paris-Orleans Railway pointsman's cabin, doing duty until a suitable prototype is found.

Shunting away three freshly painted Glyncorrwgs.

Broken windows, and pigeons on the ledge.

That young lad trespassing again. The tramplates are visible behind him.

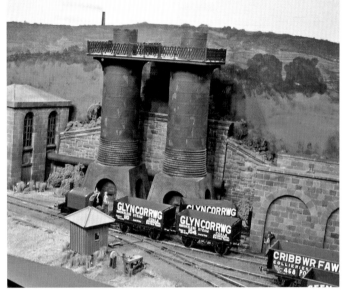

A view of the furnaces.

A view of the whole track layout. In the foreground a three-throw turnout saves space. The track is code 100 bullhead rail laid in S Scale Society chairs to Scale-seven standards – well to the extent that such a yard observes standards.

Gillan & Brown *Created by Romiley Methodist Railway Modellers*

Photos by Nigel Hart
Description by John Rodway

Engineers to the World (in miniature)

Gillan & Brown represents part of an industrial complex as it might have been in the 1960s. It was inspired by the Injector Works of Davies & Metcalfe – a once internationally renowned company in steam circles. Its headquarters used to stand across the road from the clubroom.

Operation

Every move is made either to bring in raw materials and coal, or to take out finished product and rubbish to/from the off-stage exchange sidings, just like a real factory. There are some 80 individual loads, most made from found objects (=rubbish). Their appearance is determined by a randomised card system. The Load Wrangler then has to find suitable wagons while the Drivers work them to the designated siding.

Apart from coal, all loading/unloading of wagons takes place out of public sight within buildings. The hidden sector plates give access to the backstage storage sidings. The mineral wagons are end-tipped using a tipper track and a hands-off unlatching mechanism. The coal is represented by black aquarium gravel.

Buildings

All but two building are scratch-built. There are an estimated 10,000 individually-laid slates on the roofs. Even though the buildings are in a range of architectural styles, they use a limited palette of colours so as to give coherence to the scene.

Because the back road is on a slight curve, many of the buildings have trapezoidal footprints. The tops of some buildings are removed for storage. This allows them to overhang the rear of the baseboard, giving the impression that it is wider than it really is.

Some demountable buildings straddle and mask baseboard joints. Doors in the buildings allow loads to be surreptitiously placed on/removed from the platforms. Every room that is illuminated has something inside to see, though not always what might be expected. Some whole buildings and roofs lift off so that children and those in wheel-chairs can see the interior detail.

The attention of the audience is drawn away from the exit to the long sector plate by the internally illuminated overhead walkway, the pipe bridge, and the electric light signal. The signal only changes aspect when (a) the sector-plate is in the correct position and (b) the fiddle yard operator pushes a button to indicate the route is clear. There is a repeater signal on the back of the buildings for the benefit of the drivers. The signal next to the door to the small sector plate only turns green when the door is fully up.

A 'modesty screen' clips to the baseboard frame behind this sector plate to hide the sight of operators' abdomens when the door is up.

Track

Hand-built track and pointwork. A rotary switch controls the motors of the tandem point. Micro-switches below the baseboard detect the lie of each point and cut power to the other point motor if its movement would result in a clash of point blades.

Unusual features

Dedicated story-tellers explain what is going on. There is a mirror on the floor so the audience can see the underside of the central baseboard if they lift the curtain. There are many small details for the observant to find. Some are quite incongruent and often raise a smile.

Tea break time.

A view along the full length of the layout.

Another load to the despatched.

No. 8 takes a breather.

Tipping a coal load into the basement cellar.

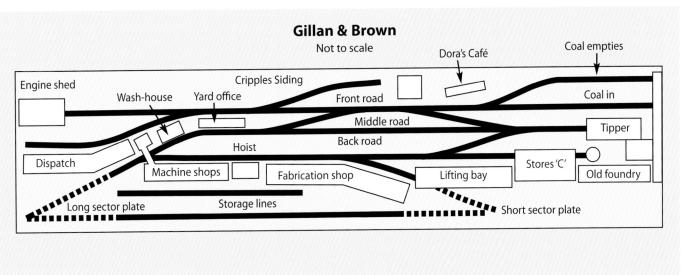

Gillan & Brown
Not to scale

Dora's Café

Coal empties

Engine shed

Cripples Siding

Wash-house   Yard office

Front road

Coal in

Middle road

Tipper

Back road

Hoist

Dispatch

Stores 'C'

Machine shops

Fabrication shop

Lifting bay

Old foundry

Long sector plate   Storage lines

Short sector plate

Bont Faen *by Derek Mundy*

Photographs by the author

Taff Vale Railways in the 1920s

As a Welshman, my railway interest reflects my parentage and it is difficult to ignore the attraction of pre group liveries of the railways which served the coalfields of South Wales. My particular favourites are the Taff Vale Railway and The Barry Railway. A contrast of lined black for the Taff and lined out Claret for the Barry.

I chose the Town of Cowbridge, Bont Faen in Welsh meaning Stone Bridge, which lies in the Vale of Glamorgan in South Wales, some twenty miles to the west of Cardiff and was initially served by the Taff Vale Railway. Artistic licence allowed me to incorporate the Barry into the plan.

During the time of the building of the South Wales Railway, which formed the basis of the Great Western in these parts, Cowbridge found itself isolated. In 1860, the local Corporation initiated a bus service to connect the town to Llantrisant, on the South Wales Railway main line. A bus service also ran to Cardiff twice weekly, taking four hours for the twenty mile journey!

A bill was passed in the House of Lords in 1862 for the construction of the Cowbridge Railway. First trains ran to Llantrisant in 1865. The railway was almost immediately operated by the Taff Vale, which connected with the GWR Broad Gauge. In 1923 over 66,000 tickets were sold from Cowbridge, equating to 220 journeys per day.

The passing of the Road Traffic Act in 1920 spelt the gradual death knell of the passenger service, with its ultimate demise coming in the wake of the Beeching report in the 1960s.

The layout

The layout shows part of the locomotive servicing facilities of the Taff Vale railway, which existed at the early station prior to the extension of the line to Aberthaw.

A single line runs along the backscene of the layout to what would have been the original station. This is serviced by the steam Railmotor No 9 and also the newly arrived loco propelled railcar TVR No 79.

All of the coaling of locomotives was carried out by hand, which involved double handling from an open coal wagon, on to a stage and then up into the loco bunkers. Locomotive ash was similarly deposited into wagons by hand shovels, to be taken away for use in line maintenance.

Underneath view of the baseboard construction method.

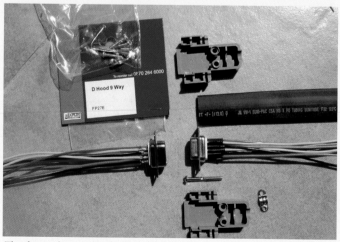

The electrical connectors between boards.

The coaling stage with recently topped up TVR loco in the foreground.

This process gives a lot of reason for moving full and empty coal wagons, on and off scene and also for the disposal of full ash wagons. A gas tank wagon also arrives, attached to a passenger service and has to be moved to a dead end siding. Full and empty coal wagons are dealt with to provide sustenance for the loco arrivals.

Both Taff and Barry engines call in for servicing and depart for duties elsewhere. A two road loco shed and a timber built coaling stage together with a couple of water columns are all the facilities needed to keep the show moving.

Construction

The baseboards were built using 9mm MDF, as this provides a good surface for track laying. The frames were made from 6mm birch ply sides and 9mm birch ply ends and cross braces. I bought in a sheet of Birch ply from a timber yard in Nantwich, who obligingly cut it into strips for me, to a plan, which gave me a stock of ply to use for a number of projects. Pattern makers dowels locate the ends. Additionally, 6mm bolts and wing nuts pull it all together. At one time, I used luggage catches but find that bolts and wing nuts are better.

Trackwork was made from Timber Tracks bases and C & L chair fittings at

31.2mm for the crossing gauge clearances. Turnout blades and all other gauge is at 32mm.

The pre-made and pre-painted track work was then glued to thin foam underlay from Hobby Holidays and ballasted with fine granite chips. Buildings are from plastic sheet to my own scale drawings, taken from photographs of the age, c1920.

A backscene bolts on to the back edge of the layout, and this has been painted in acrylics by me. It has a basis of sky which then has contours of the countryside and a townscape worked into it. Run up a few sketches to start with and locate them on the back boards with blue tack, to gauge the effect.

Operation

Sadly, I do not have a great deal of time nor the space to leave the layout erected at home, so it is left to exhibition outings to get a feel for operation. Locos and stock get the occasional run at Llanbedr group and Borders meetings, to keep the wheels turning. I do get a great deal of pleasure from building the layout and locos and stock to run on it. It's size of eleven feet overall may well suit some who have a spare room to allocate to such a project. Allow a small prototype to inspire you!

Overall view of the layout.

Courcelle Part *by Richard Chown*

Photographs by the author

Central France cameo

This layout was designed and built as a Guildex competition entry, for a layout in the limited space of 2002 square inches. It also acted as a test track for a larger project.

The design presents a cameo scene in a busy corner of a large station: what we would understand as the end of the Down Yard where train engines, both goods and empty passenger, uncouple and run round, and where there are also some goods sidings to shunt. That the yard is much larger is shown by the point lever numbering, but nothing ever passes the exit signal. A Pacific or a Mountain could run, and would not look out of place, but could not do very much.

The location is fictional, somewhere in the Haute Auvergne of France, where the Paris - Orléans and the Paris - Lyon - Méditerranée Railways met, the date being about 1880. Remember that une cour is a yard and un celle is a big fiddle.

The layout is built to O Gauge Proto43,5 standards, known in Britain as Scaleseven. The PO locos and *Marianne* are scratch-built, the larger PLM loco is built from a DJH/Model Loco kit and the smaller PLM loco was actually made in France. The vehicles are a mostly scratchbuilt, with a few kits. The autocouplings are Richard Tarpie's Lincs, thoroughly recommended as the most successful and reliable, and least visible. All the locos are fitted with the Pacific Fast Mail analogue synchronised sound system, now over forty years old.

For a layout built as a one-off, it has been to many exhibitions, and not just in the UK.

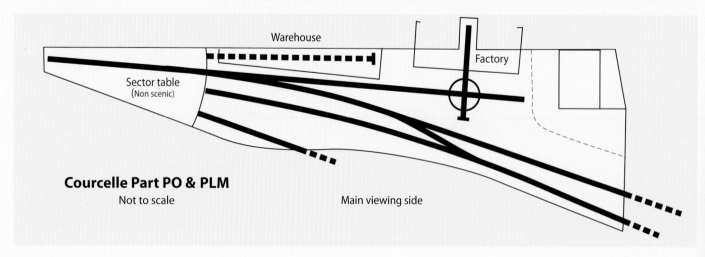

Courcelle Part PO & PLM

Not to scale

Main viewing side

Warehouse

Sector table
(Non scenic)

Factory

Tanat Valley III *by Peter Drost*

Photographs by the author

Mid Wales branch in Scale7

When I decided to change from 4mm to 7mm Scale I wanted to achieve certain criteria, GWR obviously, Welsh hopefully, small enough to fit in my car, be easy to operate for guest drivers, different and if possible and to a better standard than that I had ever achieved previously. Having seen a fine S7 layout and had discussion with the operators I plumped for that as a standard. I had in stock wheels and motor suitable for a small locomotive and to limit my losses if it did not work out. I did some research and came up with ex-B&E 0-6-0 1376 which I found had spent a lot of time on the Tanat Valley branch in Mid Wales. At about this time I had sight of Mike Lloyds all embracing book on the Tanat Valley. The die was cast. So on with the facts.

It was only after about 50 years of dodging, weaving, prevaricating and delays that this little line was opened in 1904 by which time any chance of being a success had faded and after a life of not quite 50 years it was closed. But it had become a magical byway for modellers because of the esoteric range of oddball little locomotives etc. This is my third essay about this line. Based this time on

a fictional branch from Penybont Fawr, South for about 2 ½ miles to Hirnant, where a huge natural and planted forest area several miles in each direction was exploited for the First World War effort. The original site being very restricted was expanded after the war, using three tandem points, to accommodate the development of the hughely successful 'Welsh Black' match factory.

This current layout has been built as an entry to the S7 Challenge 33 competition. Track is hand made to 7 standards using code 90 FB rail – slightly overscale but less floppy to lay – fixed to 2mm ply sleepers with copper U-clips. These pass up through the sleeper and are crimped around the rail foot, thus stimulating spiked track. All laid on 2mm cork (floor tile). Ballast is hand sifted stone dust to get the correct size.

Buildings are all hand-built with ply bases covered with plastic or card. Electrics are DC and basic, gates, loco shed doors and points operated by sub base rodding. Scenery is polystyrene carved to profile – messy but it suits me – coated with tinted and glue laced poly filler with flock grass and stone dust for roads and yard surfaces.

The layout fits the boot of my car – just!

Overall view of the layout.

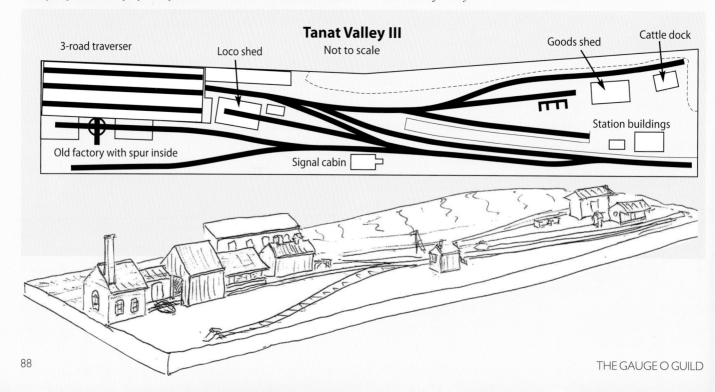

88

THE GAUGE O GUILD

Brinklow *by Pete Waterman and friends*

Photographs by Pete Waterman
Description by Mike Marritt

West Coast Mainliine in the 1960s

Most O gauge modellers will have heard of the magnificent model of Leamington Spa that has been built over the last fifteen or so years by Pete Waterman and his group of friends. For those who have had the privilege of visiting it in situ it probably remains one of the most iconic O gauge layouts they have seen, Others will have become aware of it through the many articles in the model railway press, or through the many YouTube videos that are around, or through the books Pete has written about it.

What is less well known is that part of the layout does not model either Leamington, or indeed the Great Western main line at all. In a rather remote part of the railway room is a full scale model of Brinklow, in fact according to Pete it is the only part of the railway that is fully to scale length. For those who may not know, Brinklow is a station on what we now call the West Coast Main Line, (previously the LNWR main line) situated between Rugby and Nuneaton in the West Midlands. It is at one end of a long length of straight line, which is reasonably flat. This means it is something of a race track for the trains travelling over it, and even in steam days speeds of up to 100mph were often achieved by the crack expresses of the time.

My reason for including the layout in this book is that back in the 1950s in my youth, like Pete, I was a regular visitor to Brinklow station. At the time I lived about 15 miles away, but I was lucky enough to have a next door neighbour who shared my love of railways, and on occasion he would take me by car on a summer evening to watch the succession of named expresses thundering through Brinklow. The names are still in my memory. 'The Merseyside Express', 'The Irish Mail', 'The Shamrock', 'The Mancunian', 'The Emerald Isle Express', and others. It was a very romantic period in the history of British railways.

It was visiting Brinklow, and several other main lines on the British railway system that inspired my love of models of the real thing, a love that continues to this day. And I have to say that Pete and the team have caught the true presence of Brinklow as it was sixty or so years ago.

In many ways, Brinklow is the embodiment of what many of us try to accomplish in our modelling. It has an Up Fast and Up Slow lines, and Down

Fowler 4MT 2-6-4T travels southwards on a local passenger train.

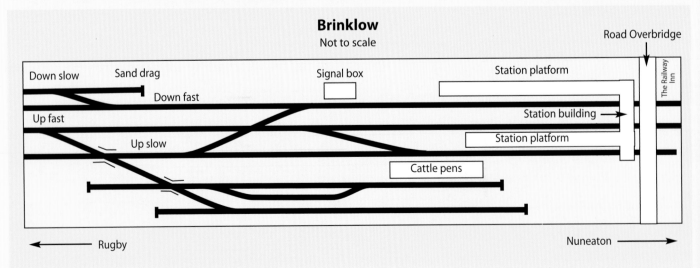

Brinklow
Not to scale

Road Overbridge

Down slow | Sand drag | Signal box | Station platform | The Railway Inn

Down fast

Up fast | Station building

Up slow | Station platform

Cattle pens

← Rugby | Nuneaton →

The cattle pens on a quiet day.

Cattle wagons awaiting their load.

Fast and Down slow lines, which means that as well as fast expresses, modellers can run local passenger services and also slow goods and mineral trains, all in an authentic setting. The goods yard and cattle dock add to the interest, enabling shunting to take place, and the track plan enables stock from these two to be despatched in either direction by way of the cross overs. The goods shed for the model is built, but at the time the photos were taken, was not in position. Pete admits that this part of the layout has not yet been developed as much as the area around Leamington station, so there is much outstanding work to be done, although the basics, station, signalling, landscaping etc are all in their setting. Due to the remoteness of this part of the layout, a video link is in place which enables the operators to keep check on what is happening.

The layout has been powered by DCC from its inception, and Pete and the team employ modern technology wherever possible. There are team leaders for every aspect of the layout building and operating. Each team consisting of three or four specialists in their field.

Sadly I do not have the time or space to accommodate a Leamington Spa in 7mm, but I could quite easily find space for a Brinklow, or similar. Layouts like Brinklow can inspire any aspirational modeller who takes the time and makes the effort to study the area, the surrounding landscape, and the traffic on the line. It certainly inspires me. Personally I do not have the skills to model to the standards of Pete and the team, but like most of us I aim to do my best.

The four track main line looking south.

The ramp up to the cattle pens.

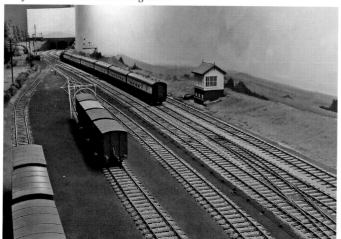
The goods yard, awaiting the installation of the goods shed. A local passenger train heads for Rugby.

The 4MT prepares to pull away.

The Summit *Yeovil Model Railway Group*

Photographs by Steve Flint courtesy of Railway Modeller
Description by Bob Alderman

Settle & Carlisle in the 1960s

The Summit was inspired by the Ais Gill section of the Settle and Carlisle line. It features the viaduct, cross-over and the two lay-by sidings for freight trains. It is fully and correctly signalled for late LMS, early BR period.

The layout showcases YMRG member's models running in a prototypical setting. There are ten coach expresses hauled by Duchesses and Deltics to local three coach passenger trains with a 4F. Large freight trains hauled by 9Fs or Super Ds. Smaller ones too. LNER locos make a showing too. The period is from before nationalisation to well into BR. This follows the member's enthusiasms. The aim is that the trains should look correct in the setting.

The layout is large. It is 47ft long by 33ft wide. One side carries the scenery and the other the fiddle yard. The scenery is extensive. The fell extends for nearly six feet behind the railway and three in front. All the control is out of sight and the railway runs without apparent human intervention apart from the signalman located at the front of the layout operating a Modratec lever frame.

The planning for the railway began in around 1995 but did not come to fruition until 2005 when we had a clubroom that could accommodate it. All the design work from track plan, basic baseboard structure and scenic area was done by our late member Brian Draper. We had the basics up and running just before Brian died. Sadly he did not see it. The layout was completed just in time for it to be exhibited for the first time at Guildex, 2015.

The scenic track is laid on a spine of conventional baseboards constructed from 12mm plywood. On the scenic areas we have used C&L plain track and their chairs and sleepers for the point work. This has been ballasted with Woodland Scenics ballast. Three colours were mixed together to achieve the effect we wanted. The fiddle yard boards are a series of table tops again in 12mm ply. The plain track here is Peco and the point work is all rail soldered to copper-clad sleepers. When built all the points were operated by Fulgarex motors but have been replaced by servos. The signals are driven by servos. The servo drivers for these have been changed from those originally fitted too.

The signals have been constructed from Scale Signal Supply components. All but one accurately reflect the signals that were once at Ais Gill. One has been changed to a bracket post to reflect its sighting on the model but otherwise follows the prototype.

A driver's eye view from ex LNER V2 Class No. 60809 The Snapper *of approaching ex LNER L1 Class No. 67760 with a local passenger train.*

Train control is by two Helmsman 5 Amp units (supplemented by stand-by controllers built by one of the members) for the Up and Down lines. These also control the Up and Down fiddle yard lines. As a train departs the fiddle yard section, switches on that line can be depressed to advance the next train to head of the storage line. There is sufficient power available to run two trains simultaneously. This feature was going to be automated but fingers on push buttons work equally well.

As the front of the layout is invisible to the two operators at each end of the layout four small video cameras relay the view of the front to each. The signal aspect can just be made out on the two monitors beside each panel but aspect repeaters on the panels ensure there should be no errors. The monitors also show the lay-by sidings so that when a train is signalled to use them the operator

The prototype Deltic *at The Summit.*

can see the position of the loco relative to the signal; similarly the guard's van relative to the siding entry and the loco once the train is in the siding.

The dramatic feature of this layout is the size and height of the scenery. It drops the railway into the countryside. Besides the track-side scenery the other scenery is made up from a series of panels of various sizes; notionally the larger ones around 5ft square and up to 2ft deep to the rear and 2 to 3 ft deep by 5ft long at the front. All have been made to be as thin as possible. They are shaped to fit against the track boards. One board is unique. This one carries the viaduct. It is an independent structure mounted on wheels. A lot of the drama of the scene is achieved by having the boards at an angle to follow the slope of the fell.

These boards are of lightweight construction. One person can lift them but their size makes it a two person job. The base material is a paper based honeycomb panel (used as a protector on a palleted load). It is 1 inch thick with similar core cell size. It can be cut with a jig saw or knife. These panels are set in a 6mm ply frame that defines the board edges. Contours within the board are created either by partially cutting through the panel and bending it or joining panels offset one to the other. These tend to be facets.

The panels are initially attached to the ply frame and one another using a hot glue gun. The joints are then completed using strips of newspaper glued to the panel and the frame. This is on both sides. The joints between panels in the frame are similarly treated.

The faceting is removed in places by adding balled up newspaper covered with further newspaper strips to round out the surface. This has also been used to redefine other surfaces to create rock faces.

The whole surface has two layers of newspaper glued on. This is then covered with earth coloured Artex. The Artex is used to for the detail of the rock faces in appropriate places.

This seemingly vast area of scenery has been simply finished. Hanging basket liner from the roll has been torn up and glued down for the majority of the grass. Some long strands needed subsequent trimming with an electric hair trimmer. Other grass and foliage is from the Woodland Scenics range. As the lining material is rather dusty the whole has been fixed with a fine spray of diluted acrylic matt medium. This serves as a further adhesive.

Notable in the scene are the drystone walls; over 100ft on the layout. Needless to say they are not laid in individual stones. The method was to stick a strip of corrugated card, corrugations vertical, onto the scenery. This was temporarily pinned with cocktail sticks whilst the glue dried. DAS modelling clay was rolled out to a thickness of about 3mm and cut into strips. The strips were stuck onto the card with pva glue. The strips were then

The viaduct, based on the one at Ais Gill, with Stanier Pacific 4-6-2 46220 Coronation *in charge of an express working.*

Cravens Class 105 DMU about to pass the sidings whilst ex LNER Class A1 Pacific No. 60128 Bongrace *heads a passenger train in the opposite direction. Note the ewe in the 6ft way oblivious to the danger.*

impressed with stone pattern. Blocks of 20mm Styrofoam about 30 × 50mm were cut and the surface was touched by a hot soldering iron. The foam recedes into a small hollow under the heat. A number of hollows were created in the stone pattern.

The blocks were then pressed into the DAS, one each time simultaneously leaving the stone pattern proud on the surface. The capping stones were made by sticking a sausage of DAS onto the top and then a blade pressed in to make individual upright stones. Once the DAS has hardened it was painted with an emulsion base coat and then patch painted the stone colour. (See the Gauge O Guild *Gazette* Vol. 19, No7, page 22 for an illustrated article on this)

BR class 9F No. 92214 passes Draper's Sidings with a lightly loaded freight working.

Another view of the 46220 Coronation *on the viaduct.*

There are few structures on the layout. The scenic part of the line is completed at each end with tunnel mouths. These are based on Birkett tunnel, a typical Settle and Carlisle tunnel profile. The road bridge at Ais Gill has also been used at one end of the railway. The signal box that once stood there, is from a Modelex etched kit, cut and shut to suit. (The original box has been relocated to Butterly at the Midland Railway Centre). The platelayers hut is based on photographs of the one that once stood there; the toilet and coal store are a surmise. They should be there but don't seem to appear in any photos. All these structures have been built from plasticard.

The layout is lit with led strips. Two colours are used; bright white and warm

A parcels working headed by a Brush Class 31 (Heljan RTR) passes under the road bridge with a parcels train. The bridge is based on the one at Ais Gill and is scratch-built from plastikard.

Fast and slow. LMS rebuilt Royal Scott Class No. 6147 The Northamptonshire Regiment *with a train of LMS coaches passes ex LNER (GER) J15 Class No. 65480 with a mixed freight, which includes a narrow gauge loco on a flat truck as part of the load.*

white. The strips are self-adhesive and stuck into white uPVC ogive guttering to make a light unit. The guttering makes a simple lightweight shade. The led's are powered from salvaged PC stabilised power supplies. Each lighting unit is suspended from tubular steel supports cantilevered over the layout from behind. These supports are also used to hold the supports from which the background sky is hung. With the high scenery this completes the sealing off of the operators.

It was always intended that the layout should be exhibited in spite of its size. To take the layout to an exhibition all the boards are packed onto specially constructed stillages. These have been constructed from square steel tube, bolted and welded together. Each board has a unique position in the its stillage. The whole layout can be packed into a 7.5 ton truck though the stock has to travel in two cars.

See www.ymrg.co.uk and www.facebook.com/yeovilmodelrailwaygroup.

Ex LMS Class 2P 4-4-0 No. 40697 on a local train of non-gangwayed coaches.

The Summit (Draper's Sidings) signal box.

LNER Class 04 (ex GCR) leaving the tunnel. This model is based on the preserved loco of this class which can be seen at Loughborough.